HOLY LANDS OF ABRAHAMIC RELIGIONS

A BRIEF HISTORY AND PILGRIMAGE

K Ravindran

notionpress.com

INDIA · SINGAPORE · MALAYSIA

ISBN 979-8-88869-630-9

Contents

❖ *Contents* ❖

❖ *Contents* ❖

Foreword

Dr. (Fr.) Joseph Valiamangalam SJ
Rector (Emeritus)
Gujarat Vidya Deep Seminary
Sevasi, Vadodara

ROSARY HIGH SCHOOL
Pratapgunj, Vadodara 390002

Foreword

World religions bear witness to the experience of Ultimate reality to which they give various names such as Brahman, God, Allah or the Absolute. Faith is accepting and responding to the Ultimate Reality. Humans experience separation from the Ultimate Reality or God which causes suffering and alienation. Religion is derived from the Latin *religere* meaning to bind or connect. Thus, religions enable the humans to experience liberation from human suffering and to be united with the Ultimate Reality or God/Allah.

Religion meets the natural adult human needs, the kind of which if not met, can turn us into sick human beings. Human beings have the need to trust that there is an enduring meaning for their individual lives and for the life of humanity as a whole. We have to be able to feel that when we try to live good lives, when we try to reach out to our fellow human beings in love and sharing, and co-operation, we need to feel that we are in harmony with the way life and the universe are made to work.

The psychologist William James defined religion as "the feelings, acts, and experiences of individual men in their solitude, so far as they apprehend themselves to stand in relation to whatever they may consider the divine". By the term divine James meant 'any object that is godlike, whether it be a concrete deity or not' to which the individual feels impelled to respond with solemnity and gravity. the theologian Paul Tillich, faith is 'the state of being ultimately concerned', and religion is simply whatever matters most for a person. Religion is the substance, the ground, and the depth of man's spiritual life.

The Swiss psychiatrist Carl Gustav Jung based on his own experience and from working with his patients, asserted that the deeper meaning necessary for carrying on the struggle of life was 'imprinted' within the unconscious depths of every person; He also realized that persons discover this deeper meaning through symbols and myths by which persons come into contact with this ultimate reality we call God. He realized that it is in the religions of the world that humanity finds the most effect set of myths and symbols to feel and discover this mystery. Thus, we can claim that religion can and make important contributions to the psychological health and productivity of a person's life. Religion functions through a blending of individual and community experience. It is a community of people searching for and living out what matters to them most.

There are three principal ways in which individual faith finds community support and expression, and so forming religion. We can name them as creed, code, and cult or ceremony.

The heart of religion is a person's own experience of God, or one's own experience of Enlightenment. What we feel in our spirit, we need to express with our body. When we share, or communicate to others, so that they also can see and share, and support what we have experienced, which gives birth to religious creeds. Many times, these are expressed through stories, myths and symbols. So in Judaism and Christianity, we find the myths of creation of the world, the flood, the escape from Egypt, and the birth and death of Jesus of Nazareth. People reflect about the meaning of these stories in an intellectual and clearly defined terms. These statements of meaning become part of the belief system, or the creed or doctrine of a particular religion.

Religious experience is expressed within a community not only through creed and doctrines, but also through moral behaviour. And so, all religions have some form of moral guidelines or ethical codes for the community in the area of human conduct, such as the Ten Commandments of Judaism and Christianity.

In every religion, religious experience is expressed not only in moral action but also in ritual action. Ritual expresses the experience in celebration or by enacting the experiences. Coming together in synagogues, churches or mosques, the believers enact, remember and celebrate through ritual, the original experience. These are passed on and made real again in the lives of the members of the community from generation to generation.   . ..

The religions that originated in the Middle East, in Palestine and the Arabian Peninsula, "the Abrahamic religions." All of them recognize the Jewish Patriarch Abraham as a key figure in their own self-understanding. Among these three religious traditions, Judaism is the parent religion, whose unity and identity were forged in the exodus event, the escape from slavery in Egypt. Jesus of Nazareth, born as a Jew preached the arrival of the Reign of God and was seen as a threat to the established Jewish religious authorities and was crucified. His followers believe that he has risen from the dead, have spread Christianity as a new religion. The faith and leadership of Prophet Muhammad gave birth to Islam during the eight century as a monotheistic religion among the Arab tribes and as a reform of Judaism and Christianity. For all these religions, God is a God of love and justice who loves humanity and calls humans to a new life of obeying God's commandments, loving, trusting God and loving each other.

To be religious today in a world of religious pluralism, to be religious necessarily we need to be inter-religious, respecting the other religions and relating to members of other religions. This will lead to peace and harmony in a society torn by religious fundamentalism and the consequent violence and destruction. Better knowledge of other religions will help us to cultivate this positive attitude towards other religions.

The present book by Wg Cdr K Ravindran (Retd) is very helpful to understand the religious traditions of Judaism, Christianity and Islam. The author has done extensive research to understand the historical development of these religions. As he writes in the Preface, he has made every effort to present the book in an objective and unbiased manner. The narrative skills of the author will help the reader to understand the sequence of events in the formation of these religions and struggle of the Jews to establish the modern state of Israel as their homeland. The second part dealing with the scriptures and worship practices of Jews and

Christians is very informative and will help the reader to get deeper insights into these religions.

The chapter on the chronological timeline on development and evolution of Judaism, Christianity and Islam is very useful as a point of reference.

Pilgrimage is considered a way in which humans strive to connect to the divine Reality and live in harmony with themselves and their environment. Most religious traditions consider the pilgrimage having a central role in religion. The author has recognized the importance of pilgrimage and so he concludes the book with a chapter giving an exhaustive itinerary of a nine-day pilgrimage tour of all the holy places associated with the Jews, Christians and Muslims. The author himself had toured with a group of Christian pilgrims and had taken extensive diary notes during the tour, which has helped him in the compilation of this itinerary.

It gives me special joy to present this book, "Holy Lands of Abrahamic Religions", and I appreciate the noble motivation of the author to present this book to the readers who are open to understand and appreciate the contribution of the world religions to human life of harmony and peace between followers of various religions since we are all fellow pilgrims on the path of God realization. It is my earnest wish that this book may contribute significantly in our common effort of building a better India and a better world in the third millennium.

Dr. Joseph Valiamangalam SJ
18-11-2022

Preface

The three Abrahamic religions trace their common patriarch to Abraham, as referred to by Jews and Christians and Ibrahim as referred to by Muslims. The origin of all three religions was in the West Asian region around Israel/Jerusalem. The West Asian region has been a flash point from prehistoric times and it continues to be so even in the present times. Volumes have been written by various theologians, historians and religious scholars of many countries on the genesis of the reasons and why periodically conflicts keep recurring there. Quite a few chroniclers have narrated the events starting from God's creation of the world, as per Judaism and Christianity. In spite of this, a layman will find it quite difficult to follow the events. The reason for this is not far to seek. Starting from the Middle Period of 2200 BCE till the 21st century, a span of over 4000 years, with multiple nations, religions, ethnicities and races battling out their differences and viewpoints almost continuously, with few periods of peace and stability in between, it is quite a Herculean task for any chronicler to cover the period in an objective manner.

For ease of understanding, the author has first given a brief narrative of the events from genesis till the formation of the modern state of Israel. The various city states involved in the wars and plundering, scattering of Jews from their homeland of Israel, Arab/Islam rise and conquest of Israel, semitism, antisemitism, claims and counterclaims of Jews/Christians and Muslims of the scriptures and their common holy lands are all included in this. The second part deals with the various holy books, scriptures and worship practices of Jews and Christians. The third part exclusively chronicles the meteoric rise of Modern Israel in all spheres against multiple odds and hostile Arab nations surrounding the newly formed state, including the disgruntled and hostile Palestinians living within Israel, after losing their statehood, zionism and antizionism.

For a quick reference to a lay reader to understand the sequence of events, a chapter on the chronological timeline on development and evolution of Judaism, Christianity and Islam has been added. Lastly, a full chapter at the end gives an exhaustive itinerary of a nine-day pilgrimage tour of all the holy places associated with the Jews, Christians and Muslims. The author had gone with a group of Christian pilgrims for this tour and maintained diary notes during the tour, which helped in the compilation of this itinerary.

The author has painstakingly tried to present the book in an unbiased and objective manner, considering the extreme sensitivity and volatile nature of the subject matter. In spite of the sincere efforts of the author, if any unintentional errors have crept in, the same may be pardoned by the readers.

– Wg Cdr K Ravindran (Retd)

e-mail ID: ravi7931@gmail.com

Acknowledgements

The efforts for compiling this book were commenced by me some years ago. It was then kept in the backburner for a long time awaiting proper research on many aspects of the contents. The research work took time and only now I have been able to complete the manuscript.

In the compilation of this book, I am grateful to my two sons, Rohit and Rahul, both abroad, for their valuable tips on various aspects covered in parts of this book. These resulted in improvement in chronicling and proper sequencing of the contents of the book. Help was rendered by Rahul for compilation of the glossary as well.

I am grateful to revered Dr. (Fr) Joseph Valiamangalam SJ for graciously writing the Foreword to the book. He is a well- known theologian and has been the Rector of Gujarat Vidya Deep Seminary for the last many years. I offer my heartfelt thanks and gratitude to him for taking time off to write the Foreword to this book, despite his extremely busy schedule.

Last, but not the least, I acknowledge my sincere gratitude to Notion Press, Chennai for prompt publishing of the book.

Vadodara, India
Dated: 19/11/2022   Wg Cdr K Ravindran (Retd)

Chapter 1

Introduction

It is quite interesting to note that historically, all ancient religions were founded, evolved and thrived only in certain specific regions of the world. Three Abrahamic religions of Judaism, Christianity and Islam trace their patriarch as Abraham and were founded in the Middle East/West Asian region of Jerusalem and Mecca-Medina. Four religions of Hinduism, Jainism, Buddhism and Sikhism were founded in India. Zoroastrianism and Baha'i were originated in Persia (present Iran). Confucianism and Taoism (or Daoism) are China based and Shintoism is Japan based. During the bronze age period of 3300 to 2200 BCE, ancient civilizations took root in the areas where human settlements had taken place. These were the cradles of the first civilizations of the world and were along the perennial river basins or seafronts. Making of bronze vessels, agricultural practices, use of potter's wheel and trade were started during this period. Egypt along the River Nile, Mesopotamia Sumer, Babylonia (present Iraq), Assyria, Turkey and Persia (Iran) along Rivers Tigris and Euphrates, Rome, Israel and Greece along Mediterranean Sea are examples of Middle East/ West Asian civilizations. Similar civilizations developed in Central Asia, South Asia and China as well during the same period. Naturally their beliefs, faiths, worship, way of living, common language, culture and customs shaped these religions. Later on, many missionaries and human movements and subsequent settlements spread these religions to other far off regions where they thrived.

Before the Advent of Religions

In the ancient period, before the advent of organized religions, people lived in various isolated pockets in the form of clans, tribes, ethnicities and social groups. These were based on their common language, customs, culture, living habits, beliefs in certain norms, worship of certain pagan gods, fear and faith on certain natural phenomena such as lightning, thunder, storm etc. which they could not comprehend or explain. They interacted socially and intermarried also among their own clans or tribes. They were fiercely independent and suspicious of anybody outside their own groups. Many such powerful clans/ tribes/ethnicities tried to subjugate other nearby clans or tribes, particularly if they were considered weak and rich. These resulted in rival clashes, killing, plundering, looting and enslaving the losers.

During the prehistoric era, the formidable kingdoms of the Middle East/ West Asian region were Romans, Greeks, Egyptians, Assyrians, Babylonians and Jews. All these kingdoms except Jews were polytheist, worshipping their own gods/idols. The Romans worshipped Jupiter,

Juno, Roma, Venus and Minerva. The Greeks worshipped Helios, Athena, Apollo, Zeus and Aphrodite. The Egyptians worshipped the sun god Ra and the king of living Osiris. The Assyrians worshipped Ashur. The Babylonians worshipped Mardak and seven other deities. Amongst all these idol worshippers, the only group who practised exclusive monotheism were the Jews. Moses who received the tablets of the ten commandments had strictly prohibited the Jews from idol worship. The Jews were allowed ritualistic animal sacrifice, incense burning and sprinkling blood to dissuade them from idol worship. In the midst of these powerful neighbouring idol worshipping city states, as the only group of monotheistic state, it was natural that the Jews faced animosity, hatred and hostility. Added to that, the Jews also faced jealousy from its neighbours due to their considerable riches of Solomon's temple. As a result, the Jews in Jerusalem frequently faced attacks from these hostile neighbours. The powerful Roman kings had always wanted to attack the wealthy Jews of Jerusalem and subjugate them. This resulted in permanent animosity between Roman kings and Jews of Jerusalem. During the period between 950 BCE and 550 CE, the neighbouring city states were always attacking each other.

During the reign of David and his many successful war campaigns, vast riches were amassed. With these, his successor son Solomon built the first Jewish temple at Jerusalem and regular temple worships started with animal sacrifices at the altar. After the death of Solomon there were many internal feuds which encouraged the neighbouring regimes to attack Jerusalem. There were serious conflicts between Babylonians and Jews from 606 to 586 BCE. During this period, the Babylonian King Nebuchadnezzer repeatedly attacked Jerusalem, plundered the city and exiled the Jews to Babylonia.

Chapter 2

Genesis to Modern Period: A Brief Narrative as per Old and New Testaments

Genesis

According to Genesis, God created the world in six days and rested on the seventh day, known as the Sabbath day. Adam and Eve were created by God and lived happily in the Garden of Eden. Satan in the form of a serpent tempted Eve to taste the forbidden apple leading to all the evil problems of mankind. Adam and Eve begot two sons, the elder Abel and the younger Cain. Out of jealousy, Cain killed Abel. Later, Cain married the daughter of Nod of the neighbouring country. The progeny of Cain indulged in a lot of sinful activities through generations, incurring the wrath of God. Noah, a pious old man of 500/600 years, was ordered by God to make a huge Ark in which he was told to collect and accommodate one pair each of all species. During the devastating deluge that took place thereafter, mankind and all animals and birds in the Ark thus survived.

According to Torah (also called Pentateuch), the most sacred book of Judaism, around 2200 BCE, God first revealed himself to a Hebrew man named Abraham, considered to be the first prophet and founder of Judaism. Abraham lived in Canaan with his wife Sarah who could not bear him a child for many years. They had an Egyptian slave called Hagar (also called Agar), who worked as maid to Sarah. On the pleading of Sarah, Abraham lived with Hagar for ten years and she gave birth to a male child named Ishmael, when Abraham was 86 years old. After another 13 years, Sarah conceived and bore a child named Isaac, when Sarah was 90 years old and Abraham was 100 years old. The young Hagar used to taunt the elderly Sarah nursing her child. Both Hagar and Ishmael were driven out from the household by Abraham due to the insistence of Sarah. They went away to the neighbouring country Arabia. The progeny of Isaac is considered to be Jews and the progeny of Ishmael is believed to be Muslims, though the actual Muslim religion of Islam was founded much later on, by Prophet Muhammad in 622 CE.

God wished to test Abraham's faith in Him and asked Abraham to sacrifice his beloved son Isaac. When Abraham took Isaac to the Temple Mount in Jerusalem, bound him and was lowering the sword, God provided a ram as substitute which Abraham sacrificed. This is the Jewish version as per the Old Testament. In the Islamic version, when Ibrahim (As per Islam the common patriarch is referred to as Ibrahim) was ordered by God to sacrifice his son, while lowering the sword, God provided a substitute goat which was sacrificed by Ibrahim. The Muslims commemorate this sacrifice as Bakrid. These two conflicting versions by Jews and Muslims are the genesis of all the hatred, animosity, disputes, conflicts and fights between them.

Exodus

Isaac's son was Jacob. Jacob had many sons through his two wives (both sisters). Joseph, one of the youngest, was very pious and good and was the favourite of Jacob. Out of jealousy, Joseph's brothers threw him into a well and presumed that he was dead. But Joseph was alive and was rescued by an Egyptian who took him to Egypt. The bright and brave Joseph went on to become a commander in Egyptian Army. Meanwhile, famine spread in Israel. The brothers kept going to prosperous Egypt and Joseph kept giving them provisions. Since Joseph recognized his brothers, he told them all to come permanently to Egypt. Thus all the brothers and many others from Israel migrated to Egypt. After the death of Joseph, all those who migrated from Israel were made slaves by the Pharaohs for building their grand pyramids for the next 400 years. The Israelis were highly fertile and were multiplying too fast. The Pharaohs were afraid that the quickly multiplying Israelis would join enemy forces and defeat them. The Pharaohs therefore ordered that all Israeli male children would be killed immediately after their birth. Due to this edict, when child Moses was born, the mother put the infant in a basket to float along a river. The father of Moses was Amran. Moses had two siblings, an elder brother named Aaron and a sister named Miriam. The queen of Pharaoh picked up the infant and brought him up along with her son prince Ramses.

When the two became adults, Moses came to know that he was an Israeli. He joined the slaves building the pyramids for the Pharaohs and rebelled against the ruling Pharaoh. He led all the slaves out of Egypt through the parting of Red Sea into the Sinai Peninsula. In Sinai, leaving the followers, Moses went up the mount for praying and communicating with God. Through the "burning bush", God talked to him and gave him the tablets of the Ten Commandments. The English version of these commandments are reproduced below:

Thou shalt have no other Gods before me

Thou shalt do no idol worship

Thou shalt not take the name of the Lord in vain

Thou shalt remember the Sabbath day

Thou shalt honour thy father and thy mother

Thou shalt not kill

Thou shalt not commit adultery

Thou shalt not steal

Thou shalt not bear false witness against thy neighbour

Thou shalt not covet anything that is thy neighbour's

In the prolonged absence of Moses, many followers turned disbelievers and started merrymaking, praying to a golden calf idol made by them. Upon his return with the tablets, Moses was horrified to see this idol worship by the disbelievers and cursed them. Leading the faithful followers, he wandered in the wilderness of the deserts for the next 40 years and reached Mount Nebo in the present Jordan. There Moses got the vision of God who showed him the "Promised Land" in the valley in front, which is the present Israel with Jerusalem at its heart. God also told Moses that he would not reach the "Promised Land". Moses died in Mount Nebo at the age of 120 years and it is believed that he was buried somewhere in Mount Nebo area by God Himself. But the burial grave of Moses has not been seen by any human. This story of the exodus of Israelis from the slavery under the Pharaohs, believed to have taken place around 1250 BCE, is beautifully captured in the Hollywood magnum opus "The Ten Commandments" by Cecil B DeMille.

King David

The first king of Israel was Saul. He ruled around 1050 BCE. God was displeased with him and decided to anoint a commoner as the next king. God chose David, a shepherd, for his extreme devotion to God and the love with which he tended his flock of sheep. The people of Israel were living in fear due to a giant named Goliath, who was terrorizing them. Once when Goliath challenged a crowd in Jerusalem area, David accepted the challenge. Goliath mocked at the puny David. With a single sling shot, David killed Goliath. He became an instant hero and was taken into Saul's army. With his skills and bravery, David won many battles and soon became a commander in the army. Saul's son prince Jonathan was very friendly with David. King Saul became jealous of David due to his popularity. In a battle Jonathan got killed and soon David was anointed king around 1010 BCE. He ruled for next 40 years. The first 8 years he ruled from Hebron in Judah and the next 32 years, from 1002 to 970 BCE, from Israel. He built the city of David south of the Temple Mount in Jerusalem. David was very talented and always had his harp by his bedside. He had composed 150 psalms. He was keen to build a grand temple in the name of God. But God refused to let him do so, as he was a man of war and his hands were soiled with too much of blood in the various battles he fought. However, during his long reign, he amassed vast amounts of gold, silver, bronze and other resources for building a temple, which he wished his son Solomon to build.

King Solomon

David's son Solomon succeeded him in 970 BCE. God offered him three boons and against all three he wished for wisdom only, and God was pleased to grant same. During his reign, he gave many well-known decisions including the most quoted one of dividing in two an infant claimed by two women. He thus became known as Solomon, the wise. He ruled Israel for 39 years till 931 BCE. As per the wish of his father, he built a magnificent temple and a royal palace in 7 years from 958 to 951 BCE on the Temple Mount with the altar of sacrifice at Moriah. Moriah is the place where Abraham was ordered by God to sacrifice his son Isaac and where David had already erected an altar of sacrifice. Jews consider Moriah as the only place where they can offer sacrifice in accordance with Pentateuch or Torah, which consists of the first five books of the Old Testament. This first temple was built by Solomon with the locally available rocks and limestone and the timber/logs of cedar supplied by the king of Lebanon through the Mediterranean Sea route.

The queen-wife of Solomon was Naamah, the daughter of Pharaoh of Egypt, whose influence turned him to an idol-worshipper against the wish of God. Solomon had 700 wives and another 300 concubines. The wealthy kingdom of Sheba, mentioned in Old Testament, is considered to be the South Arabian Sheba in Yemen or Ethiopia or Egypt. The Queen of Sheba was a contemporary of King Solomon around 950 BCE. Though dark by complexion, she was strikingly beautiful. She had heard lots of stories about Solomon's wisdom and was keen to meet him. She visited the kingdom of Israel with a caravan of camels loaded with jewellery, spices and other gifts for Solomon. Solomon extended a lavish hospitality on her visit. She tested Solomon's wisdom and got convinced about his just reputation as Solomon, the wise. After remaining as the honoured royal guests for some period, she and her entourage/retinue of soldiers and courtesans returned to Sheba with many return gifts from Solomon. There are some legends describing the birth of a son through the union of Solomon and Sheba. This son and his progeny are believed to have established a dynasty in Ethiopia, first of Jews and then of Christians, for over 2,000 years till the last Emperor Haile Selassie was overthrown in 1974 CE.

Division of Israel, Banishment/Scattering/ Diaspora of Jews

The original Jews consisted of 12 tribes. These 12 tribes were named after the 12 sons of Isaac's son Jacob, who was later named Israel after whom the country is named. After the death of Solomon in 931 BCE, there were many succession problems. In a civil war between 926 and 922 BCE, Israel was divided into Northern Kingdom of Israel with Samaria as its capital with 10 tribes and Southern Kingdom of Judah (or Juda in Latin and Greek and Judea, Judaeau or Judaea in Hebrew), with Jerusalem as its capital, with the two tribes of Judah and Benjamin. Both Samaria and Judah are part of West Bank of Jordan. Judah area includes Jerusalem, Bethlehem, Jericho and Hebron. For the next over 200 years, Israel remained divided. Later on, from 606 to 586 BCE, Israelis were banished/exiled to Assyria, Babylon and further, in the first exile, and from Israel to many countries in the world from 135 CE onward in the second exile called scattering or "diaspora". The 10 tribes, which got scattered all over the world, are known as the lost tribes of Israel.

King Herod, the Great

King Herod lived from 74/73 to 4/1 BCE and reigned Jerusalem from 37 to 4/1 BCE as a vassal king of Rome. He was reputed to be quite brutal and ruthless and had passed the edict to kill all new-born infants when the oracle told him that his enemy was born in Jerusalem. The Archangel Gabriel told Joseph and Mary to flee with baby Jesus to escape the wrath of the king.

Herod was known as a great builder. On Temple Mount in Jerusalem between 37 and 4 BCE, King Herod built a new enlarged temple over the one built by Zerubbabel, after erecting a platform over the existing temple and erected walls around the temple as well. Also, between 25 and 13 BCE, at the site of a port city built earlier by Greeks and Romans, he built an ambitious and spectacular port city with harbour, warehouses, markets, wide roads, baths, temples and public buildings by bringing water to the city through aqueducts. He named the new city Caesarea in honour of the Roman Emperor Augustus Caesar. The magnificent ruins of this city can still be seen. For these reasons he is referred to as King Herod, the Great.

Jesus and New Testament Events

Most historians believe that Jesus was a real person who was born between 2 BCE and 7 BCE. Much of what scholars know about Jesus comes from the New Testament of the Christian Bible. According to the text, Jesus was born to a young Jewish virgin named Mary in the town of Bethlehem, south of Jerusalem in modern-day Israel. Christians believe the conception was a supernatural event, with God impregnating Mary via the Holy Spirit. Mary's husband, the "earthly" father of Jesus, was a carpenter.

Very little is known about the childhood of Jesus. Scriptures reveal that he grew up in Nazareth, he and his family fled persecution from King Herod and moved to Egypt. After around 4 years or so, they returned to Jerusalem and Jesus was circumcised and dedicated in the temple. At the age of 12 years, Jesus visited the temple and later pronounced judgement in the temple. Jesus was raised Jewish, and according to most scholars, he aimed to reform Judaism—not create a new religion. When he was around 30 years old, Jesus started his public ministry after being baptized in the River Jordan by the prophet, known as John the Baptist. For about three years, Jesus travelled with 12 primary disciples (also known as the 12 apostles), teaching large groups of people. Christianity began as a Second Temple Judaic sect in the 1st century CE in the Roman province of Judea. Jesus's apostles and their followers spread around Syria, the Levant, Anatolia, Mesopotamia, Transcaucasia, Egypt, Ethiopia and Europe. It soon attracted gentile God-fearers, which led to a departure from Jewish customs, particularly after the fall of Jerusalem in 70 CE which ended the Temple-based Judaism. Initially, due to persecution by Romans, Christianity remained an underground religion by practitioners for almost three centuries. The Roman Emperor Constantine, the Great, converted to Christianity in 312 CE and decriminalized it in his empire. Early Christianity was consolidated into what would become the state church of the Roman Empire allowing Christianity to flourish.

According to the Bible, Jesus was arrested, tried and condemned to death. Roman governor Pontius Pilate issued the order to kill Jesus after being pressured by Jewish leaders who alleged that Jesus was guilty of a variety of crimes, including blasphemy. Jesus was crucified by Roman soldiers in Jerusalem, and his body was laid in a tomb. According to scripture, three days after his crucifixion, his body was missing. After the crucifixion and resurrection of Jesus in 29/30 CE, the pilgrims who had assembled for the Pentecost on Mount Zion saw the Holy Spirit coming and enveloping them. Jesus also appeared to his disciples at Galilee and the mountain. According to popular belief, after 40 days from the day of resurrection, Jesus finally ascended to heaven from the site of the Church of Ascension at Mount of Olives.

It is generally accepted that Jesus lived for 33 years. Many scholars believe Jesus died between 30 CE. and 33 CE., although the exact date is debated among theologians. But because of the difference between lunar calendar of Julian and solar calendar of Gregorian, the exact period when Jesus lived is disputable. Julian calendar was introduced in 46 BCE by the Roman ruler Julius Caesar. Gregorian calendar was introduced in 1582 CE by Pope Gregory XIII. The Gregorian calendar is a refinement of Julian calendar and is the present universally accepted international calendar. However, the general consensus is that Jesus was born between 6 and 4 BCE and was crucified between 29 and 33 CE. Therefore, the CE period does not commence with the year of birth of Jesus.

Emperor Hadrian

Hadrian lived from 76 to 138 CE and ruled Rome from 117 to 138 CE. He was a just and able administrator and his reign was known for peace and prosperity. He was also a great builder. He rebuilt the Pantheon in Rome, which was earlier destroyed by fire. He constructed the temples of Venus and Roma. He also built Hadrian's wall in north Britain, marking the northern boundary of Roman empire. He loved Greece and contributed to many projects there. In his honour, Hadrian's Arch was constructed by the Greeks in Athens. He visited Jerusalem which was in ruins then, with the second temple on Temple Mount (reconstructed by Zerubbabel) set to fire and totally destroyed by the Roman General Titus in 70 CE. He built a new city there and also constructed Hadrian's Arch on Mount Zion at the "Via Dolorosa". But when he built a temple dedicated to Jupiter at the site of Solomon's temple, there was a Jewish rebellion resulting in war with the Romans. In 135 CE, Hadrian defeated the Jews, banished them from Jerusalem, executed the Jewish scholars and carried out a public burning of Torah, the sacred Jewish religious books. The Jews were again exiled from their homeland, resulting in their diaspora to faraway places.

Change of name from Israel to Palestine

Hadrian gave the name Palastina to Israel area, so that the Jewish identity was totally wiped out. Hadrian also renamed Jerusalem as Aelia Capitolina. The name Palastina was derived from Peleshet and came to be known as Philistine or Falastin and later as Palestine. The original inhabitants of Philistine were neither Semites or Hebrews nor Arabs and had no connection with Arabia. Thus, Palestine has never been the name of a nation or state. It is a geographical term used to designate the region at those times in history when there was no nation or state there.

Emperor Constantine

Constantine lived from 272 to 337 CE and was the Roman Emperor from 306 to 337 CE. His mother was Queen Helena. He was the first Roman emperor to claim conversion to Christianity along with his mother after he won a decisive war subsequent to appearance of Jesus in his dream. Through an edict in 313 CE, he allowed tolerance of Christianity which was for three centuries surviving in catacombs (underground tunnels) right from the time of Jesus. Constantine built a new imperial residence at Byzantium and renamed it Constantinople (present Istanbul) after his name. This Byzantine empire lasted over 1000 years. On his orders and along with his mother Queen Helena, the Church of the Holy Sepulchre was built over the purported site of Jesus' tomb in Jerusalem next to the Temple Mount. This church has become the holiest place in Christendom. He is known as Saint Constantine, the Great, of the Eastern Orthodox Church.

Emperor Justinian

Justinian lived from 482 to 565 CE and was the Byzantine emperor from 527 to 565 CE ruling from Constantinople. He is known as Saint Justinian, the Great, of the Eastern Orthodox Church. He was a great builder and under his orders, the magnificent Hagia Sophia Church was constructed between 532 and 537 CE. With its massive dome, it is considered to be an epitome of Byzantine architecture and served as a model for many buildings constructed later on. It served as the Eastern Orthodox Cathedral and the seat of the Patriarch of Constantinople from 537 CE till 1453 CE, except between 1204 and 1261 CE, when it was converted by the Fourth Crusaders to a Roman Catholic Cathedral under the Latin Empire. He constructed a nunnery at St. Catherine in Mount Sinai where the remains of St. Catherine of Alexandria were believed to have been deposited by the angels after her martyrdom in Alexandria. He also built a chapel at the "Burning Bush" nearby.

Semitism and Antisemitism

Semitic literally means "Relating or denoting to the peoples who speak Semitic languages". The Semitic languages refer to a family of languages that include Hebrew, Arabic, Aramaic and certain ancient languages such as Phoenician and Akkadian, constituting the main subgroup of the Afro-Asiatic family.

However, the word antisemitic refers to hatred, discrimination or hostile actions mainly against Jews. It is called "the world's oldest hatred" and its history goes back many centuries. The word antisemitism was popularized by the German journalist Wilhel Marr in his polemic "The Victory of Jewry over Germandom", published in 1879. He said that it was born of the immutable and destructive nature of the Jews and their "tribal peculiarities" and "alien essence".

Antisemitism could be categorized into three stages: "ancient or pre-Christian antisemitism, which was primarily ethnic in nature; Christian antisemitism, which was religious in nature and the modern antisemitism of the 19th and 20th centuries which is racial in nature". In practice, it is difficult to differentiate antisemitism from the general ill-treatment of nations by other nations before the Roman period, but since the adoption of Christianity in Europe, antisemitism has undoubtedly been present. The Islamic world has also historically seen the Jews as outsiders. The dawn of the Scientific and Industrial Revolutions in 19th-century Europe bred a new manifestation of antisemitism, based as much upon race as upon religion, which culminated in the Holocaust that occurred during Hitler's Nazi period culminating in World War II.

The formation of the state of Israel in1948 caused new antisemitic tensions in the Middle East. The seemingly endless conflicts in the Middle East have made the problem worse as they spawn divisive domestic politics in the West. What we are seeing is an ancient and deeply embedded hostility towards Jews that is re-emerging, as the barbarous events of World War II recede from our collective memory. The American historian Joshua Trachtenberg, writing during World War II, noted: "Modern so-called 'scientific' antisemitism is not an invention of Hitler's. It has flourished primarily in central and eastern Europe, where medieval ideas and conditions have persisted until this day, and where the medieval conception of the Jew which underlies the prevailing emotional antipathy toward him was, and still is, deeply rooted".

Origins of Christian Antisemitism

Anti-Semitism has existed to some degree wherever Jews have settled outside Palestine. In the ancient Greco-Roman world, religious differences were the primary basis for anti-Semitism. In the Hellenistic Age, for instance, Jews' social segregation and their refusal to acknowledge the gods worshipped by other peoples aroused resentment among some pagans, particularly in the 1st century BCE–1st century CE. Unlike polytheistic religions, which acknowledge multiple gods, Judaism is monotheistic—it recognizes only one God. However, pagans saw Jews' principled refusal to worship emperors as gods as a sign of disloyalty.

Although Jesus of Nazareth and his disciples were practicing Jews and Christianity is rooted in the Jewish teaching of monotheism, Judaism and Christianity became rivals soon after Jesus was crucified by Pontius Pilate, who executed him according to contemporary Roman practice. Religious rivalry initially was theological. It soon also became political.

Historians agree that the break between Judaism and Christianity followed the Roman destruction of the Temple of Jerusalem in the year 70 CE and the subsequent exile of Jews. In the aftermath of this devastating defeat, which was interpreted by Jews and Christians alike as a sign of divine punishment, the Gospels diminished Roman responsibility and expressed Jewish culpability in the death of Jesus both explicitly (Matthew 27:25) and implicitly. Jews were depicted as killers of the Son of God.

Christianity was intent on replacing Judaism by making its own particular message universal. The New Testament was seen as fulfilling the Old Testament (the Hebrew Bible) and Christians were the new Israel, both in flesh and in spirit. The God of justice had been replaced by the God of love. Thus, some early Church Fathers taught that God had finished with the Jews, whose only purpose in history was to prepare for the arrival of his Son. According to this view, the Jews should have left the scene. Their continued survival seemed to be an act of stubborn defiance. Exile was taken as a sign of divine disfavour incurred by the Jews' denial that Jesus was the Messiah and by their role in his crucifixion.

As Christianity spread in the first centuries CE, most Jews continued to reject that religion. As a consequence, by the 4th century, Christians tended to regard Jews as an alien people who, because of their repudiation of Christ and his church, were condemned to perpetual migration. This belief was best illustrated in the legend of the "Wandering Jew". When the Christian church became dominant in the Roman Empire in 4th century, its leaders inspired many laws by Roman emperors designed to segregate Jews and curtail their freedoms when they appeared to threaten Christian religious domination. As a consequence, Jews were increasingly forced to the margins of European society.

Brief History of Temple, Western Wailing Wall, Church, Mosques and Hadith/Sura/Miraj

1. The Jewish Temple: Construction, Destructions, Reconstructions, Enlargements and Burning

As per the wishes of King David, his son Solomon, constructed the first Jewish temple on a magnificent scale on Temple Mount in Jerusalem in seven years from 958 to 951 BCE. In 586 BCE King Nebuchadnezzar of Babylonia burnt Jerusalem and destroyed this temple. In 515 BCE. Nehemiah and Zerubbabel reconstructed the temple. Between 37 and 4 BCE, King Herod built a new enlarged temple over the one built by Zerubbabel, after erecting a platform over the existing temple and erected walls around the temple as well. In 70 CE, General Titus of Rome laid siege to Jerusalem and destroyed the city and set fire to the temple.

2. Western Wailing Wall

The Western Wailing Wall at Temple Mount is considered to be the holiest and most sacred place for all Jews. Only a part of the ancient wall survives today. One has to pass through the Jewish quarter of the old city of Jerusalem to enter the wall. There are separate sections of the wall for men and women. Before proceeding to the wall, one has to wash one's hand and collect a skull cap which is to be worn over the head. All Jews wear a black hat and a black overcoat over a white dress. On the wall, there are many crevices/recesses where they can deposit slips of paper after writing their wishes on them. It is believed that such wishes are fulfilled after one prays at the wall and deposits the slips of paper. The Jews stand facing the wall and wail to express their sorrow and deep anguish on the destruction of the ancient temples built/rebuilt/enlarged by Solomon/Zerubbabel/King Herod and the mosques built over the temple site by Muslims.

3. The Church of the Holy Sepulchre

After Christianity was recognized by Emperor Constantine in 313 CE, he and his mother Queen Helena built the Church of the Holy Sepulchre in 325-326 CE, adjacent to the site of the destroyed Jewish temple on Temple Mount, at the site where Jesus was crucified and buried.

4. The Mosques/Domes

After the death of Prophet Muhammed in 632 CE, Muslims captured Jerusalem in 636 CE. Between 688 and 691 CE the mosque with dome of black rock was built by Caliph Abd al Malik at Temple Mount in Jerusalem. It is believed to have been built over the site of the temple built/rebuilt/enlarged by Solomon/Zerubbabel/King Herod. The mosque, known as Haram al Sharif, meaning "Noble Sanctuary", is considered a holy shrine of Islam.

Nearby, to the east of this mosque is the "dome of chain", which is open all around, built in 691 CE, by same Caliph Abd al Malik. The site of the dome of chain is considered to mark the exact centre of Temple Mount.

It is neither a mosque nor a shrine, but is used as a prayer house by Muslims. According to Islam belief, on Judgement Day, the chain hung from the centre of the dome would stop the sinners from passing through and let only the just pass through. According to Jewish belief, the dome of chain was used by King Solomon to test the persons who appeared in his court to settle disputes. He asked them to hold the chain. Those who would give false witness would be struck by lightning passing through the chain, while those who spoke the truth would leave unharmed. In later period, repairs of the dome of chain were carried out by Mamluks and Ottomans.

In 705 CE, a bigger mosque with golden dome was built just to the east of the dome of chain. Originally, it was built as a small prayer house by Rashid un Caliph Omar and later it was rebuilt and completed by his son al-Wahid in 705 CE. The golden mosque was built at the purported site of a visit one night in 621 CE by Prophet Muhammad, who referred to his visit to the Temple Mount site as Al Aqsa, meaning "the farthest". Thus, the mosque with the golden dome is known as Al Aqsa mosque and is considered to be the third holiest mosque of Islam. The largest and holiest mosque of Islam is in Ka'aba at Mecca, known as Masjid al-Haram (called The Grand Mosque) where at the holiest cuboid shrine, Hajj is performed by all Muslim pilgrims. The second holiest mosque of Islam is at Medina known as Al-Masjid an-Nabaur (Mosque of Prophet) where Prophet Muhammad was buried.

5. Hadith/Sura/Isra/Miraj

Hadiths are collections of reports, accounts or narratives purporting to quote what Prophet Muhammad said verbatim on any matter. They are second only to Qur'an in developing Islamic jurisprudence. Sura is a chapter of Quran. Isra and Miraj are two parts of a journey which Prophet Muhammad undertook around 621 CE. It is described as both a physical and spiritual journey by Muhammad during a single night on his flying steed Buraq, which he tethered on a pole at Temple Mount. He then went to heaven, where he speaks to God and receives instructions to take back to the faithful, regarding the details of the prayer. He returned next morning, held prayers with his followers at the Temple Mount and left for Mecca. He referred to the visit to the Temple Mount site as Al Aqsa, meaning "the farthest". In Sura 17 Al-Isra of the Qur'an, a brief sketch of the journey is given, while other details are in the Hadiths.

Crusader Kingdom Period

In 1099 CE, the crusaders captured Jerusalem from Muslim control and used the Al Aqsa mosque as a palace, the mosque of black rock as a church and the dome of chain as a chapel. During the Crusaders' Kingdom period in the 12th century, churches were rebuilt in the area of the Church of the Sepulchre and worship by Christian pilgrims restarted and continued during the millennium. The crusaders were in control of Palestine till 1187. Later on, between 1192 and 1291, the crusaders exercised control over Palestine intermittently due to takeover by Muslim rulers in between.

In 1187 CE, the great Muslim conqueror and founder of Ayyubid dynasty Salah-ad-Din Yusuf ibn Ayyub of Egypt (also called Saladin) captured Jerusalem from the crusaders and restored the two mosques. Both the mosques are considered quite sacred to Muslims. More repairs and renovations were carried out on both mosques by Ayyubids, Mamluks and Ottoman Turks in later periods.

Ottoman Period

By 1300 CE the Byzantine empire became quite weak. The Ottoman empire was founded by Osman I in 1300 CE. After Sultan Mehmed II conquered Constantinople in 1453, the state grew into a mighty empire. The Ottomans captured Jerusalem in 1517 CE. They constructed walls around the old city of Jerusalem and built the neighbourhood. In the later period, maintenance/repairs of the mosques were carried out by the Supreme Muslim Council of Palestine and Jordan and in the present period they are administered by the Islamic Waqf Board of Palestine and Jordan. Waqf board in Islam oversees the property dedicated to religious endowment such as a building or plot of land for religious or charitable purposes. It can be a mosque, tomb, graveyard or religious school/Madrassa.

With the conquest of Constantinople by the Ottomans, Hagia Sophia was converted into an imperial mosque and remained so till 1931 CE. It was the most important mosque of Istanbul till the equally magnificent Sultan Ahmed mosque was built in 1616 CE, just adjacent to Hagia Sophia. With its blue dome it is known as the Blue Mosque. The apex of the empire was reached under Suleiman, the Magnificent, in the 18th century when it stretched from Persian Gulf to Hungary and from Egypt to Caucasus. From 1908 the decline of the empire started with the Young Turk revolution. In World War I the Allied Forces defeated the Ottomans and the empire was dismantled in 1918. The Young Turk revolution culminated in the abolition of the Ottoman Sultanate in 1922.

Mustafa Kemal Ataturk

Mustafa Kemal Ataturk lived from 1881 to 1938. He was a Turkish army officer and revolutionary. He founded the Republic of Turkey in 1923 and was its President from 1923 till his death in 1938. In 1924 he abolished the Caliphate and the Sharia courts. He modernized Turkey by making it democratic and secular. He gave equal rights and status to women, reduced the burden of taxation on peasants and established schools with free and compulsory education. He was a visionary who turned Turkey into a modern nation of the 20th century.

Mustafa Kemal Ataturk is also known for secularizing Hagia Sophia by converting it into a museum. Since then it remains one of the most visited tourist attractions in Istanbul.

British Period and Creation of Israel

In 1917 during the end of World War II, the British forces under General Allenby captured Palestine defeating the Ottomans. From 1922 to 1947, the British ruled Palestine under a mandate from the League of Nations. Frequent clashes between Arabs and Jews took place in Palestine during this period. World War II raged between 1939 and 1945 when holocaust of Jews by Germans took place. In 1947, the UN General Assembly adopted a resolution for partition of Palestine, providing the establishment of a Jewish state of Israel by dividing Palestine between Jordan and Israel, with part of Jerusalem with Israel and the remaining part of Jerusalem and West Bank of Jordan River with Jordan. In 1948, the Republic of Israel was proclaimed.

After the six - day war of 1967 between Israel and the Arabs and the many local conflicts at Temple Mount, a truce was agreed upon between the two sides according to which Jerusalem would be under Israeli control and the two mosques would be under Waqf Board control. As per the agreement, non-Muslims including Jews are permitted to enter the compound of the mosques and freely move around, but they cannot enter the mosques or pray there. Only Muslims are allowed entry into the two mosques.

"Homecoming" of Jews

With the open immigration policy adopted by the newly created nation, vast numbers of the diaspora of Jews spread all over the world were invited to come and settle in the

"Promised Land" of Israel, termed "Homecoming". Many Jews from the European countries responded to this call and came and settled in Israel. 500,000 Jews from Russia and 16,000 Falasha Jews from Ethiopia migrated to Israel in 1992 and became Israelis. In recent times, some Jews in the north-eastern state of Mizoram in India claimed to be from the 12 lost tribes of original Israel. They were allowed to migrate to Israel after verification of their dialects, customs and rituals by Rabbis from Israel.

Chapter 3

Contradictory Claims and Counterclaims in Abrahamic Religions

All the three Abrahamic religions of Judaism, Christianity and Islam, trace their ancestry to Abraham. Also, all three religions were founded in the West Asian region. Both Jews and Muslims believe in their common ancestor-prophets with Muslims having slight variations in the names. According to one version of Islam, there are six prophets (Jewish English names shown within brackets) - Adem (Adam) whose wife was Hawwa (Eve), Nuhh (Noah), Ibrahim (Abraham), Musa (Moses), Isa (Jesus) and sixth and the last Muhammad. They also believe in Shaytan (Satan), Imran (Amram), Harun (Aaron), Ilyas (Elijah), Idris (Enoch), Jibril (Gabriel), Mariam or Miriam (Mary) and Yahya (John, the Baptist). In Islam, sons of Adem and Hawwa are Habil (Abel) and Qabil (Cain) and sons of Ibrahim are Ismail (Ishmael) and Ishaq (Isaac). There are also many common Muslim names such as Dawood (David), Suleiman or Sulayman (Solomon), Boutros (Peter), Kader (Andrews), Adil (James), Yahya (John), Faris (Philip), Bin Fadan (Bartholomew), Ataullah (Matthew or Mattiyahu), Tau'am or Te'oma (Thomas),

Fouad (Thaddaeus), Shamoon (Simon), Yaqub (Jacob or James), Yehuda (Judah or Judas Iscariot), Isar (Israel), Mikaeel (Michael), Yusuf (Joseph), Javed (John), Yunus (Jonah), Ayyub (Job), Azar (Terah), Zakariya (Zachariah), Al-usabat (Elizabeth) etc.

According to another version of Islam, there are a total of 26 prophets. These are Adem (Adam), Seth (Seth), Idris (Enoch), Nuhh (Noah), Hud (Heber), Salih (Methusaleh), Lut (Lot), Ibrahim (Abraham), Ismail (Ishmael), Ishaq (Isaac), Yaqub (Jacob), Yusuf (Joseph), Shu'aib (Jethro), Ayyub (Job), Dhul-kifl (Ezekiel), Musa (Moses), Harun (Aaron), Dawood (David), Sulayman (Solomon), Ilias (Elias), Alyasa (Elisha), Yunus (Jonah), Zakariya (Zachariah), Yahya (John, the Baptist), Isa (Jesus) and Muhammad, being the last.

As per Judaism, there are 48 male prophets and 7 female prophetesses (Miriam, Deborah, Hannah, Abigail, Huldah, Esther and Sarah). As per Christian belief, there are 50 prophets, who are almost common to Judaism.

According to texts of Judaism, Christianity and Islam, Abraham lived in Canaan and was 86 years old when Ishmael/Ismail was born through Hagar. Hagar was an Egyptian slave and worked as maid to Sarah. Sarah could not bear a child during all the years she was with Abraham. On the pleading of Sarah, Hagar lived with Abraham for 10 years and bore the child named Ishmael/Ismail when Abraham was 86 years old. Again, all three religions agree with the version that Ishmael/Ismail was 14 years old when Ishaq/Isaac was born through Sarah and Abraham, by then, was 100 years old. To test the faith and devotion of Abraham, God appeared in his vision and ordered him to sacrifice his son. The son must have been around 5 years old since he walked with Abraham to the sacrificial altar at Moriah in Temple Mount in Jerusalem and the boy was bound before preparing to sacrifice, as per Genesis. Both Genesis and Bible say that God ordered Abraham to sacrifice "Thy only son" which clearly means Ishmael, as Isaac was yet to be born. However, Torah names Isaac as the son to be sacrificed. This was the starting point of the contradictory claims of Judaism and Islam. Further, it is believed that as God's reward, a second son was to be born to Abraham for fulfilling the order for sacrificing his only son.

As per Sura 11.71-74, Sarah was promised a son (Ishaq/Isaac) and a grandson (Yaqub/Jacob), thus excluding the possibility of premature death of Ishaq/Isaac. According to Islam, Ibrahim was to sacrifice his son at Marwah near Ka'aba, though the name of the son is not mentioned anywhere. Due to God (Allah) being pleased with Ibrahim's devotion to Him in preparing to sacrifice his only son, a substitute goat was provided to Ibrahim for the sacrifice. This sacrifice is commemorated annually by Muslims as "Bakrid". Qur'an also says – "Believe in all the books".

However, another anomaly raised by Jews is when Hagar was driven out of the house by Abraham on the insistence of Sarah, consequent to Hagar taunting Sarah for nursing the infant Isaac, why she chose not to go to where she originally belonged ie Egypt (which is much nearer than Mecca and easier to reach). According to Islam texts, on God's orders, Ibrahim left Hagar and the infant Ismail/Ishmael near Ka'aba much before the birth of Ishaq/Isaac. There in the desert, Hagar ran between hills of Safa and Marwah searching for water to save the life of the thirsty Ismail/Ishmael. When she could not get water, she prayed to God and then she found water sprouting from the earth which was scratched by the feet of Ismail. She dug around that spot which turned into a well called Zamzam from where she collected water to quench the thirst of Ismail. During the Hajj pilgrimage the pilgrims walk between the two hills of Safa and Marwah in commemoration of this event. From the perennial waters of Zamzam, the Hajj pilgrims collect the holy water and take home.

If the son Abraham had to sacrifice was Isaac, then Ismail would have been over 18 years at that time and where was he? Genesis also states that Ishmael and Isaac together buried Abraham in the cave of Machpelah in the field of Ephron.

It is also said that Jews do not commemorate specifically the sacrifice of Isaac as their festivals do not commemorate events of unique individuals. The Jews only have a festival of sacrifice called Korban, which is a festival of general application to sacrifice.

In Kiryat Arba Hebron in Palestine area, tombs of the patriarchs of Jews are located side by side. These tombs are of Abraham, Sarah, Isaac, Jacob, Rebekah, Leah etc. Nearby, in the same premises, there are parallel tombs side by side of Ibrahim, Hagar, Ishmael etc who are considered to be their patriarchs by Muslims. It is obvious that the remains of Abraham/Ibrahim cannot be in two different tombs when he is considered to be the common patriarch

It can thus be seen from the above that there are too many contradictory claims and counterclaims of the events of the ancient period resulting in acrimonious debates and accusations by both Jewish and Islamic academics, scholars and theologians of misinterpreting and even doctoring of holy texts, to justify the respective claims of the two warring religions. Despite the passage of many centuries, the acrimonious debates, controversies, claims/counterclaims and animosities still remain, with the fights continuing in the highly volatile West Asian region.

Chapter 4

Holy Books and Scriptures of Judaism and Christianity

The Hebrew Bible and the Scriptures

These consist of Tanakh and Talmud with their various subdivisions, as briefly explained below:

Tanakh

The most sacred canonical collection of Hebrew scriptures comprising the books of law, the prophets, and collected writings is known as the Hebrew Bible or the Tanakh or the Mikra. The books of the Tanakh were passed on by each generation and, according to rabbinic tradition, were accompanied by an oral tradition, called the Oral Torah. These texts are almost exclusively in Biblical Hebrew, except for some Biblical Aramaic passages in the books of Daniel and Ezra. The Hebrew Bible is also the textual source for the Christian Old Testament. The form of this text that is authoritative for rabbinic Judaism is known as the Masoretic Text and it consists of 24 books, while the translations divide essentially the same material into 39 books for the Protestant Bible. It includes the same books as the Old Testament in the Christian Bible, but they are placed in a slightly different order.

1. Torah or Pentateuch (Teaching - Books of Law)

Torah or Pentateuch, stands for Teaching which consists of five books. These are the most sacred holy books of Judaism, believed to have been written by Moses himself after Exodus. The five books are – Genesis, Exodus, Leviticus, Numbers and Deuteronomy. These first five books outline the basic laws and tenets of Judaism for Jews to follow. Genesis chronicles the events before Exodus dealing with the creation of the world by God in six days, seventh day being the rest day of Sabbath, Adam and Eve at Garden of Eden, Noah's Ark and the Great Deluge, Abraham and the sacrifice at Mount Moriah on Temple Mount, Abraham's son Isaac, grandson Jacob taking the name of Israel whose son Joseph and his brothers and followers fleeing to Egypt and awaiting their liberation through Moses from slavery of the Pharaohs.

The five books were hand-written on scrolls (specially processed parchment or animal skin) around 600 to 500 BCE.

The history of scrolls dates back to ancient Egypt. In most ancient literate cultures, scrolls were the earliest format for longer documents written in ink or paint on a flexible background. Rigid media such as clay tablets were also used but had many disadvantages in comparison. Though scrolls have long been superseded by the codex book format, but scrolls are still produced for some ceremonial or religious purposes for use in synagogues.

2. Prophets

Prophets is sub-divided into two parts: The former prophets, the books of Joshua, Judges, Ruth, Samuel and Kings are narratives that explain the history of Israel from the perspective of Israel's fulfillment of God's covenant. The latter prophets, the oracular discourses of Isaiah, Jeremiah, Ezekiel and the twelve (minor) prophets report the exhortations of these fiery leaders to return to God and Torah.

3. Writings

Writings include poetry (psalms and lamentations), wisdom/literature (proverbs and ecclesiasts), story (Ruth), short stories (Esther) and histories (Ezra-Nehemiah and 1-2 Chronicles).

Talmud (Learning)

Talmud means "Learning". The Talmud contains the Mishnah and the Gemara. Following the destruction of the Temple in Jerusalem by the Romans in the year 70 CE, Jewish religious scholars of Israel compiled the six volumes of the Mishnah in order to record and preserve the canon of Jewish religious legislation, laws and customs. During the next few centuries, this was supplemented by the Gemara, which are interpretations, commentaries, discussions and debates outlining the importance of 613 commandments of Jewish law, contributed by thousands of rabbinical scholars in Israel and Babylon. Together these two texts comprise the Talmud which remains a living source of religious study, thought and commentary. The first version of the Talmud was finalized around the 3rd century CE. The second form was completed during the 5th century CE. These are rabbinical writings in orthodox Judaism.

Maimonides – 13 Articles of Faith

Judaism embraces several other written texts and commentaries. One example is the 13 Articles of Faith, which was written by a Jewish philosopher named Maimonides. Moses ben Maimon, commonly known as Maimonides and also referred to by the acronym Rambam, was a medieval Sephardic Jewish philosopher who became one of the most prolific and influential Torah scholars of the Middle Ages. In his time, he was also a preeminent astronomer and physician.

Language

Aramaic

Aramaic is the ancestral language to both Hebrew and Arabic. It is a family of languages or dialects belonging to Northwest Semitic family of Assyria, Babylonia, Mesopotamia, Iraq, Syria, Turkey and Iran and also the Canaanite languages of Hebrew and Phoenician.

Hebrew

The official language of Jews is Hebrew. But it has the following variations:

Ashkenazim (Plural of Ashkenazi). Originally Jews of Germany, France and East European countries, but now European-American Jews also, speak Ashkenazi, a mixture of German and Hebrew. Yiddish is a variation of Ashkenazi used by central and eastern European Jews before Holocaust, but now spoken by Jews of America, Israel and Russia.

Sephardim (Plural of Sephardi). Occidental branch of European Jews who settled in Spain, Portugal, Greece, Netherlands, England and Americas speak Sephardi, a mixture of Spanish and Hebrew. But the original Spanish Jews who got expelled in 1492 and also those from North Africa and Middle East speak Ladino or Judeo-Spanish, another variation of Sephardi.

The Christian Bible

The Christian Bible is a collection of 66 books written by various authors. It is divided into two parts: The Old Testament consists of 39 books and the New Testament consists of 27 books. Testament is a covenant between God and man. The officially recognized books of Bible are known as Canons. 14 books of Bible of dubious authenticity excluded from Canons by Jews and Protestants, but sometimes printed as Appendix to Old

Testament, are called Apocrypha. A Bible containing versions/texts in different languages is known as Polyglot.

The important parts of Old Testament are Pentateuch. The five books of Pentateuch are Genesis, Exodus Leviticus, Numbers and Deuteronomy.

Pentateuch plus Joshua is known as Hexateuch

Hexateuch plus Judges is known as Heptateuch

Heptateuch plus Ruth is known as Octateuch

Heptateuch plus books of Samuel plus books of Kings is known as Enneauteuch

In case of Enneauteuch, Ruth is not included and two books each of Samuel and Kings are considered as one book each.

God's promises to man as revealed in the Bible are called Covenant

Disclosure of God's will or religious truth of Bible is called Revelations

Critical interpretation of Bible is known as Exegesis

The Biblical founder or Father of human race or Hebrew people is called Patriarch

Bible in Latin version by St. Jerome for Roman Catholics is called Vulgate

The English translation in 1610 CE of Vulgate for Roman Catholics is called Douay Bible

The English translation in 1611 CE for Anglican Church is called King James Bible

The Bible kept in all hotel rooms, distributed by an international organization, is called Gideon Bible

The New Testament was written after the death of Jesus. The first four books—*Matthew, Mark, Luke* and *John*—are known as the "Gospels," which means "good news." These texts, composed sometime between 70 CE. and 100 CE., provide accounts of the life and death of Jesus.

Letters written by early Christian leaders, which are known as "epistles," make up a large part of the New Testament. These letters offer instructions as to how the church should operate.

The *Acts of the Apostles* is a book in the New Testament that gives an account of the apostles' ministry after the death of Jesus. The author of Acts is the same author as one of the Gospels—it is effectively "part two" to the Gospels, what happened after the death and resurrection of Jesus.

The final book in the New Testament, *Revelations*, describes a vision and prophecies that will occur at the end of the world, as well as metaphors to describe the state of the world.

The New Testament, originally written in Koine Greek, contains 27 books which are agreed upon by all churches.

The King James Version is quite popular because of its striking English prose. It was translated from the Erasmus Greek Bible.

The Christian Scriptures

Christianity, like other religions, has adherents whose beliefs and biblical interpretations vary. Christianity regards the biblical canon, the Old Testament and the New Testament, as the inspired word of God. The traditional view of inspiration is that God worked through human authors so that what they produced was what God wished to communicate. The Greek word referring to inspiration is *theopneustos*, which literally means "God-breathed".

Some believe that divine inspiration makes our present Bibles inerrant. Others claim inerrancy for the Bible in its original manuscripts, although none of those are extant. Still others maintain that only a particular translation is inerrant, such as the King James Version. Another closely related view is biblical infallibility or limited inerrancy, which affirms that the Bible is free of error as a guide to salvation, but may include errors on matters such as history, geography, or science.

The books of the Bible accepted by the Catholic, Orthodox and Protestant churches vary somewhat. These variations are a reflection of the range of traditions, and of the councils that have been convened on the subject. However, there is substantial overlap. Every version of the Old Testament always includes the books of the

Tanakh, the canon of the Hebrew Bible. The Catholic and Orthodox canons, in addition to the Tanakh, also include the deuterocanonical books as part of the Old Testament. These books appear in the Septuagint, but are regarded by Protestants to be apocryphal. However, they are considered to be important historical documents which help to inform the understanding of words, grammar, and syntax used in the historical period of their conception. Some versions of the Bible include a separate Apocrypha section between the Old Testament and the New Testament.

Chapter 5

Modern Israel

Arab-Israeli Wars

Since the newly formed nation was surrounded on all sides by hostile Arab nations, fights were expected to take place. The five Arab-Israeli wars which took place during the period from 1948 to 1982 and the formation of PLO (Palestine Liberation Organization) are briefly covered below:-

1. **1948-49 War.** As soon as the British Government established Israel out of the Palestine area, skirmishes and war broke out in May 1948. Since Palestine was divided between Israel and Jordan with no independent territory for Palestinians, the bitterness and enmity were quite high. By March 1949 Israel was able to somewhat secure its borders through their military might and sheer survival instinct.

2. **1956-57 War.** Nationalization of Suez Canal by Gamal Abdel Nasser of Egypt (then known as UAR-United Arab Republic) resulted in tension and conflicts. Israel attacked Egypt's Sinai Peninsula and captured Gaza strip and Sharm-el Sheikh which is

at the southern tip of Sinai. In 1957 Israel withdrew from these two places after guaranteed access to Gulf of Aqaba, which is vital for Israel for imports from eastern countries. United Nations Emergency Force was stationed in Sinai since then to ensure this.

3. **1967: The Six-Day War of June, 1967.** This was a brief lightning surprise war fought by Israel, led by Prime Minister Yitzak Rabin and Defence Minister Moshe Dayan at the helm, with Egypt led by Gamal Abdel Nasser, Jordan led by King Hussein and Syria. The territories conquered and annexed by Israel were Gaza strip and Sinai Peninsula from Egypt, West Bank of Jordan River consisting of Judah, Samaria and East Jerusalem from Jordan and Golan Heights from Syria. Israel increased its territorial area from its original 20,800 sq.kms (8,000 sq.miles) to 62,400 sq.kms (24,000 sq.miles) at the end of the Six-Day-War. This was a record achievement for any country in history in such a short period. For the first time in 2,000 years, the Jews were in complete control of Jerusalem.

4. **1973-74: The Yom Kippur War and the Camp David Accord.** On the Yom Kippur Jewish holiday on 6th October, 1973, President Anwar El Sadat of Egypt launched a surprise attack on the unprepared Israel across Suez Canal to Israel's western border. Simultaneously, Syrians from the north launched an attack on Israel's northern border. Israel, caught by

surprise, took time to mobilize its forces, who then pushed the two enemy forces back. Ceasefire was declared between Egypt and Israel on 25th October, 1973. But fight between Israel and Syria continued till 1974 when US Secretary of State Henry Kissinger brokered ceasefire between the warring countries. In September, 1978, after 12 days of secret negotiations at Camp David in US, between Israeli Prime Minister Menachem Begin and Egyptian President Anwar El Sadat in the presence of US President Jimmy Carter, the **Camp David Accord** was signed. As per the accord, Sinai Peninsula was returned to Egypt, but Israel kept control over Gaza strip, West Bank and Golan Heights. The Nobel Peace Prize in 1978 was shared by Menachem Begin and Anwar El Sadat for the Camp David Accord. However, the UN condemned the accord since the agreement dealt with the Palestinian territories without the participation of Palestinian representatives. Islamic extremists were angry with Sadat and assassinated him in 1981.

5. **1982 War.** In 1978 the Palestinian guerrillas from their base in South Lebanon launched air raids on Israel. Israel sent troops to occupy a strip of 6 to 8 kms deep in South Lebanon to protect its border. Despite the presence of UN peace-keeping forces, occasional fighting continued. In 1982 Israel launched a massive attack and destroyed all PLO bases and laid siege on Beirut, capital of

Lebanon. A US sponsored plan was accepted by PLO and all guerrillas evacuated Beirut and went to other Arab countries. Israel withdrew from Lebanon after maintaining a permanent Lebanese-Christian- policed buffer zone at its northern border with Lebanon. In 1982 a border check post named Menachem Begin was opened between Eilat port at the southern tip of Israel and Taba of Egypt, enabling Israelis visa-free access to the holy St Catherine Monastery at Mount Sinai and the holiday resort of Sharm el Sheikh in Sinai Peninsula. In 2005, Israel withdrew from Gaza strip.

6. **Palestine Liberation Organization (PLO).** PLO was founded by the Palestinians in 1964 in Jerusalem for liberating Palestine through armed struggle. It is recognized by over 100 countries and has observer status in UN since 1974. Both Israel and US considered PLO as a terrorist organization. But in 1993 PLO recognized Israel's right to exist in peace and agreed to give up violence and terrorism. In response, Israel recognized PLO as the representative of Palestinian people. Yasser Arafat was the chairman of PLO executive committee from 1969 till his death in 2004. He is succeeded by Mahmoud Abbas, also called Abu Mazen.

Revised border map of Israel

The revised border map of Israel is given below giving details of the present - day Israel.

Population and Geography

The present population of Israel as of 2021 is around 9.4 million, consisting of 70% Jews, 25% Muslims and 5% Christians and others. Hebrew is the official language. In 1925, Hebrew University was founded at Jerusalem during the British rule. Other universities in Israel are at Tel Aviv, Haifa and Ben Gurion in Negev area. The literary rate is quite high. The Muslims speak Arabic. Complete Jerusalem, which was Palestine territory, is under Israeli military control. The present geographical area of Israel is 62,400 sq. kms (24,000 sq.miles). To ensure the safety and security of the newly founded nation against hostile Arab neighbours, all able-bodied adults, both men and women, are trained in handling of military weapons and are available at short notice for war service in case of emergency. USA, the most ardent supporter of Jewish state, has been the chief supplier of most military hardware to Israel. However, Israelis themselves have developed their own military hardware, particularly night vision equipment.

Politics

The political, legislative and judicial capital is Jerusalem and the financial centre is Tel Aviv, where most of the embassies of foreign nations are located. There are six districts in Israel – Jerusalem, Northern, Haifa, Central, Tel Aviv and Southern plus Judah and Samaria areas. East Jerusalem and West Bank of Judah and Samaria areas are not recognized by UN. Antonio Barluzzi, the famous Italian architect was the main architect for most of the pilgrimage centres restored, renovated and developed in modern Israel. The currency is NIS (New Israel Shekel) and the exchange rate, as of 2021, is 3.28 NIS for one US $ or 0.30 US $ for 1 NIS.

Community Living and Conscription

After modern Israel was founded, many Kibbutz centres (called Kibbutzim, the plural of Kibbutz) were established. These are community living centres which are self-sustained collective farming settlements, similar to the communes in Communist China. A tenure of Kibbutz living is often considered compulsory for the young generation. So is the conscription by all able-bodied citizens for military service and training in handling of military weapons for the defence of their borders against the hostile Arab neighbours all around.

Agriculture

Israelis are pioneers in developing drip irrigation as they have to conserve the scarcest commodity of water in their country. With the drip irrigation techniques, they have turned the desert into a blooming agricultural land producing dates, olives, figs, pistachios, grapes, oranges, pomegranates, apples, mangoes and all varieties of vegetables. The seven spices of the holy land of Israel are dates, olives, figs, pomegranates, grapes, wheat and barley.

Industry

Many industries have been developed by Israel, particularly diamond polishing in which they are world leaders along with India. Based on the mineral-rich Dead Sea water, many factories have been set up producing a vast array of medicinal and cosmetic goods for export purpose.

Tourism

By facilitating a tourist-friendly infra-structure, the modern Israel state has been able to attract tourists from the world over. Due to the large number of Christians spread in every continent/country of the world, the pilgrimage tourism industry is a major source of revenue income for Israel. In addition to the large number of pilgrimage sites spread all over Israel, they are spread in many parts of Jordan and Egypt as well. Excellent highways/motorways have been developed by Israel connecting all sites of pilgrimage interest, as these are approachable mainly by roads only. Israel has meticulously developed two types of tourism, one for the leisure tourist and the other for the pilgrim tourist.

1. Leisure tourism. The first area which is also developed as a popular holiday resort is the Tel Aviv-Jaffa area with its Mediterranean seafront and promenades. The beautiful beaches attract large number of holiday makers. This financial and economic centre of Israel has become a fashion centre with many boutiques, bars, clubs, shopping arcades etc.

The second site is developed on the Galilee sea front at Yigal Allon Centre. A huge area on the seafront has been developed for tourists to camp and spend some days in a leisurely manner. There are many hotels also nearby for those who wish to stay with more comfort.

The third area is near the Dead Sea called Kaliah beach front. The Dead Sea is the lowest point on earth, being at 400 m (1312 ft) below sea level. Here the tourists can enjoy floating on the Dead Sea where one cannot drown due to the buoyant heavy salty water. The tourist may also avail of the variety of cosmetic products available for skin treatment. These are manufactured out of the clay and salt from Dead Sea, known for their rich mineral content having medicinal properties.

The fourth area which has been developed for the leisure tourist is near Eilat port area, close to the road border between Israel and Egypt. Eliat port is at the mouth of Gulf of Aqaba. This seaside resort has been developed by Israel catering mainly to the big-spending leisure tourists. It has a large number of luxury hotels, huge malls, shopping centres, fashionable arcades and casinos.

2. Pilgrimage tourism. The pilgrimage tourism has become a booming industry in Israel. It has been developed by Israel attracting tourists from all over the world, visiting the large number of sites of religious and pilgrimage significance in Israel and neighbouring Jordan and Egypt. Almost all the sites associated with the religions/faiths of Judaism, Christianity, Bahai and some of the sites of Islam are located in Israel. The pilgrims generally come in groups, headed by a pastor/priest escorting and guiding the group members throughout the pilgrimage. The pilgrims come from all countries of all the continents of Europe, North America, South America, Australia, New Zealand and Asia. The Asian groups from India, South Korea, Taiwan and Philippines regularly visit the pilgrimage sites. Most of the Indian groups come from the South Indian states of Kerala, Tamil Nadu, Telangana/Andhra Pradesh and Karnataka and also from Jharkhand, Chhattisgarh and Gujarat. The groups may consist of 20 to even 60 members. With many of the groups doing prayer sessions at the pilgrimage sites, all sites are quite crowded, making it more difficult as the approaches to the sites are through narrow roads/lanes, many of them with cobbled stones. The pilgrim groups generally observe austerity/penance such as abstinence and refrain from alcohol, drugs, smoking etc.

For the pilgrim tourist, there are two popular circuits, one can choose from. In the first circuit, the group lands in Amman, capital of Jordan, visits the centres in Jordan and proceeds to Israel crossing the border check post at King Hussein Bridge over River Jordan and enters Israel. After extensively covering all the religious and pilgrimage sites in Israel, the tourist exits Israel through the Menachem Begin border check post at Taba to Egypt. They then visit the St. Catherine Monastery at Mount Sinai and proceed further through Sharm el Sheikh, travel along the Red Sea coast and enter Cairo through the tunnel across Suez Canal. In Cairo they visit the holy sites where Joseph and Mary with baby Jesus had spent some years and conclude the pilgrimage by exiting from Cairo.

In the second circuit, the groups start the pilgrimage from Cairo in the reverse direction and exit through Amman.

Symbols or Emblems of Israel

The Jewish symbols or emblems of Israel are Star of David (Magen David), The Ten Commandments and Menorah or Candelabra. The Star of David is the most popular Jewish emblem by which the modern nation of Israel is known since the flag of Israel also contains it. The Ten Commandments tablet depiction is also used as an emblem. The menorah is another symbol used in Judaism. The Hebrew word Menorah or Candelabra is a branched candlestick or lamp with seven lights and was used in Jewish worship at the Temple in Jerusalem. Though candelabrum is singular and candelabra is its plural, the word candelabra is extensively used both in singular and plural senses. These three Jewish emblems are depicted below:

Star of David (Magen David)

The Ten Commandments Tablets

Menorah or Candelabra

Zionism and Antizionism

For centuries, Jews have lived all over the world. Almost every country has its own Jewish minority. Two countries have a large Jewish community: Israel and the United States, both having a population of around 6 million each. But in the United States Jews are but a small minority. In Israel, on the other hand, almost 80% of the population is Jewish.

The United Nations supported the division of what was then still called Palestine into a Jewish and an Arab part. And they supported the creation of the new state of Israel. The state of Israel was founded after the Second World War, in 1948 in the Middle East, in a place where Jews had lived for thousands of years with their Arab neighbours. Because of their history and religion, Jews had felt a strong connection with this region for generations. Many European Jews who had survived the Holocaust, went to live in Israel after the war. Many Jews from Arab (Muslim) countries also fled or migrated to Israel.

Among the Arab population, however, there was a lot of resistance. Immediately after the creation of the State of Israel, five neighbouring Arab countries declared war on Israel. Israel won that war. Many Arab residents of the region had to flee the country. The seventy-year history of the State of Israel is characterized by the struggle with the Palestinians. They see Israel as the occupying force.

Zionism is about the pursuit of an independent Jewish state. The word is derived from Zion, a hill near the city of Jerusalem. To many religious Jews, Israel is 'the promised land'. But many non-religious Jews, too, value the fact that there is a country where Jews can live in freedom and safety. Although many Jews identify with Zionism, there are still many different points of view. That is reason enough not to mix up the words 'Jew', 'Israelis' and 'Zionists'. Nowadays, the word Zionist is often used as a swearword, as a negative label. Many Palestinians and supporters of the Palestinian cause no longer distinguish between the words 'Jew', 'Israeli' and 'Zionist'. That is not correct. Most Jews do not live in Israel. Not every inhabitant of Israel is Jewish; there are also many non-Jews living in Israel. And not all Jewish Israelis are 'settlers' who want to conquer more and more Palestinian land. The vast majority of Jews believe that the State of Israel should continue to exist. But many Jews, both living in Israel and elsewhere, are in favour of a Palestinian state alongside Israel as a possible solution to the conflict.

Anti-Zionism is opposition to Zionism. The term is broadly defined in the modern era as opposition to the State of Israel or, prior to 1948, its establishment, as well as to the political movement of Jews to self-determination. The anti-Zionism movement has attracted supporters and controversy, including within the broader Jewish community. Critics of anti-Zionism have charged it is a cover for modern-day antisemitism, that it may be motivated by prejudices against Jewish people, or that it creates a climate where antisemitism is viewed as acceptable. Defenders of anti-Zionism have rejected these characterizations and counter-accused critics of attempting to stifle legitimate criticisms of Israeli policies, particularly of Israeli military actions and occupation of the West Bank.

Chapter 6

Chronological Historical Timeline of Jews and Israel

Bronze Age: 3300 to 2200 BCE. Use of bronze and other early features of urban civilization started. Bronze, which is harder and more durable than other metals was produced by smelting copper and alloying with tin. During this period, early agriculture, potter's wheel and trade started in the cradles of earliest civilizations of West Asia, Central Asia, South Asia and China. The earliest writing systems also developed in civilizations of Egypt (hieroglyphs) and Mesopotamian Sumer (cuneiform script).

Middle Period: 2200 to 1550 BCE. Abraham, Isaac, Jacob and Joseph

Moses Period: 1550 to 1200 BCE. Joseph and many Israelis in Egypt as slaves building pyramids for Pharaohs. Moses rebelled and led followers through parting of Red Sea to Sinai Peninsula. Received tablets of 10 Commandments from God. 40 years of wandering in wilderness. Moses received God's vision of "Promised Land" of Jerusalem at Mount Nebo.

Iron Age: 1200 to 1000 BCE. Heating techniques for producing iron were developed in this period. In 1200 BCE Joshua conquered Canaan. Others are Joshua, Gideon, Samson (with Delilah, the temptress) and Deborah, the prophetess.

First Temple Period: 1000 to 586 BCE

1010 to 970 BCE. King David

970 to 931 BCE. King Solomon. First Temple built by Solomon in 951 BCE

926 to 922 BCE. Civil war. Israel divided as Northern and Southern kingdoms

910 BCE. Solomon's temple was plundered but not destroyed, by Pharaohs of Egypt.

835 BCE. Jehoash repaired the temple.

720 BCE. Ahaziah, Assyrian king of Judah, dismantled Solomon's bronze vessels to make altar

716 BCE. Hezekiah, King of Jerusalem, resisted the attempts of Assyrians to capture Jerusalem.

640 BCE. King Josiah repaired the temple.

606 BCE. The Babylonian King Nebuchadnezzar conquered Judah and Jerusalem and exiled the Jews to Babylonia, known as the first exile of Jews from Jerusalem.

598 BCE. Jerusalem was plundered by King Nebuchadnezzar a second time.

597 BCE. King Jehoiachin was taken captive by Nebuchadnezzar. A second wave of Jews exiled to Babylonia.

587 BCE. King Zedekiah rebelled against Nebuchadnezzar. Zedekiah was blinded and taken to Babylonia where he died. Zedekiah was the last king in the line of David to reign in Israel.

586 BCE. Nebuchadnezzar burnt Jerusalem and destroyed the temple. This was the destruction of the first temple. Most Jews were exiled to Babylonia.

Assyrian and Babylonian Period: 586 to 539 BCE

573 BCE. Ezekiel in Babylonia got a vision from God giving details of a future temple to be built at Jerusalem.

553 BCE. Babylonian King Belshazzar desecrated the temple vessels. Babylonia was taken over by Medo-Persian empire.

Persian Period: 539 to 334 BCE

Torah was written during this period.

539 BCE. Cyrus, the Great, the mighty Persian Zoroastrian Emperor, established his control over the Medo-Persian empire and captured Babylonia.

538 BCE. The edict of Cyrus allowed the Jews in Babylonia to return to Israel. Jews were in their land, but under Persian control.

531 to 515 BCE. Foundation for the second temple at Jerusalem laid in 531 and took 16 years to complete in 515

with an altar of sacrifice at Temple Mount, by Nehemiah and Zerubbabel.

Hellenistic (Greek) Period: 334 to 63 BCE

332 BCE. Alexander, the Great, the mighty Macedonian Conqueror, invaded Jerusalem. He was persuaded by the priests of the temple not to destroy Jerusalem and the temple.

320 BCE. Jerusalem was captured by Ptolemy Soter of Egypt.

320 to 65 BCE. Period of unrest when fights to control Jerusalem continued and Jerusalem was ruled by Greeks, Ptolemys of Egypt and Seleucids of Syria.

Roman Period: 63 BCE to 324 CE

63 BCE. Jerusalem captured by Roman General Pompey.

40 BCE. Jerusalem captured by the Parthians of Persia

38 BCE to 4 BCE. Jerusalem captured by Romans and Herod installed as vassal king. He enlarged the temple and surrounded it with walls

6 BCE to 60 CE. Jesus and New Testament events

63 to 70 CE. Revolt against Rome. Roman General Titus laid siege to Jerusalem in 70 CE, set fire to the temple and destroyed both the city and the second temple.

132 to 135 CE. Jewish revolt against Rome. Jerusalem was sacked by Emperor Hadrian, leading to the second

exile and scattering of Jews all over the world, known as "diaspora".

Byzantine Period: 324 to 636 CE

313 CE. Adoption of Christianity by Emperor Constantine. Establishment of Byzantine empire at Constantinople. Israel became Christian.

325/326 CE. Church of Holy Sepulchre built by Constantine and Queen Mother Helena at cave tomb of Jesus at Temple Mount. Worship by Christian pilgrims commenced.

Arab Period: 636 to 1099 CE

636 CE. Arab takeover of Jerusalem

688 to 691 CE. Mosque with dome of black rock built

705 CE. Mosque with golden dome, known as Al Aqsa, built

746 to 1035 CE. Two earthquakes destroyed the mosque. It was rebuilt in 1035 CE and stands till the present day.

1076 CE. Arsie of Egypt captured Jerusalem

1095 CE. Afdhal ibn Badr retook Jerusalem from Egypt

Crusader Kingdom Period: 1099 to 1291 CE

There were total 8 crusades led by the European Christian nations against the Muslims to take control of Jerusalem region from 1096 till 1291CE.

1099 to 1187 CE. First crusade leader Godfrey de Bouillon of France captured Jerusalem. Used mosque of golden dome as a palace, mosque of black rock as a church and dome of chain as a chapel. Repairs were carried out on Church of Holy Sepulchre. Pilgrimage to church restarted.

1187 to 1192 CE. Saladin, the Great, of Ayyubid dynasty of Egypt, captured Jerusalem from crusaders and restored the two mosques. More repairs and renovations carried out on the mosques by Ayyubids, Mamluks and Ottomans later on.

1192 to 1291 CE. Frequent attacks and control of Jerusalem by Khwarazmians/Mamluks and crusaders .

1291 to 1294 CE. Period of unrest with Mongols sacking Jerusalem in 1293-1294 CE.

Mamluk Period: 1294 to 1516 CE

Mamluk Sultanate rulers from Egypt recaptured Israel region, defeating Mongols. Akko (Acra) and Jaffa ports were destroyed by Mamluks for fear of invasions by new crusaders. Plague, locust invasions and earthquakes caused devastation.

Ottoman Period: 1516 to 1917 CE

1517 CE. Sultan Suleiman, the Magnificent from Ottoman Empire of Turkey, conquered Palestine. The present walls that surround the old city of Jerusalem were built. Neighbourhood was built around the Jerusalem walls. Palestine was brought under Ottoman empire.

1832 CE. Ibrahim Pasha of Egypt took over Palestine.

1840. Palestine returned to Ottomans with British intervention.

1897 CE. First Zionist Congress met in Basel, Switzerland for establishing a Jewish state in Palestine.

1914 to 1917 CE. World War I. The city of Tel Aviv was founded during the World War.

British Period: 1917 to 1948 CE

1917 CE. British forces under General Allenby captured Palestine defeating the Ottomans.

1922 to 1947 CE. The British ruled Palestine under a mandate from the League of Nations. Frequent clashes between Arabs and Jews took place in Palestine during this period. World War II raged between 1939 and 1945 when holocaust of Jews by Germans took place.

1947 CE. The UN General Assembly adopted a resolution for partition of Palestine, providing the establishment of a Jewish state of Israel by dividing Palestine between Jordan and Israel, with part of Jerusalem with Israel and the remaining part of Jerusalem and West Bank of Jordan River with Jordan.

1948 CE. Republic of Israel proclaimed

Chapter 7

Itinerary of Nine Day Pilgrimage Tour of Holy Lands

The author had taken the first circuit of pilgrimage, as mentioned under chapter on Modern Israel. A day-to-day account of the pilgrimage is given in the following paragraphs, with a brief description of the history and relevance, of each of the sites visited.

Day 1

Landed at Amman, capital of Jordan, around 1100 hours. Visited Madaba city, known as city of mosaics, inhabited for nearly 3,500 years. Visited George Church which has a 6th century CE Byzantine mosaic map showing Jerusalem and other holy sites. Visited Mount Nebo which has a memorial to Moses. It is believed that Moses was given a vision of the "Promised Land" of Israel in the Jordan valley by God from Mount Nebo, which overlooks the valley. God also told Moses that he would not live to see it. It is further believed that God himself buried Moses somewhere in Mount Nebo area, but no one till date has seen or identified the burial place.

Proceeded by road to cross Allen Bridge so named after the British General who entered from here to Palestine during World War I. This bridge has now been renamed Sheikh Hussein Bridge after the King of Jordan and is the land border check post between Jordan and Israel. A vast no-man's land is being developed at this border check post for security reasons. Stayed overnight at a hotel in Tiberias, overlooking the Sea of Galilee for two nights to visit the holy places around Sea of Galilee.

Day 2: Forenoon

In the morning, visited the Sea of Galilee. As per the map of Sea of Galilee available for buying by the tourists, Jesus is believed to have performed 12 miracles in and around the Sea of Galilee. At the entrance at Yigal Allon Centre, there is a museum where the chief exhibit is a wooden boat which remained submerged underwater in the sea for 2,000 years. It was lifted and retrieved from the seabed in 1961. Since then many more similar wooden boats were manufactured and they are now used for taking the pilgrims for boat rides in the Sea of Galilee. The Israeli government has barraged the sea with embankment to make a reservoir with filtration plant for supply of drinking water to the people. The seafront is being developed by raising the land to make a seaside resort for attracting the large number of tourists who arrive here. It is believed that in one of the miracles performed by Jesus, he had calmed a storm and walked over the seawater. The boundary between Jordan and Israel is the River Jordan which originates from the slopes of Mount

Herman, then flows into the Sea of Galilee and continues its flow further to end in Dead Sea. After the boat ride in the sea, proceeded to Nazareth, the boyhood town of Jesus where Basilica of Annunciation (meaning announcement or prediction) is built over the grotto (cave), where Archangel Gabriel appeared to announce that Mary would bear a son. Then proceeded to Capernaum, which was the centre of public ministry of Jesus after his early years in Nazareth. Here Jesus is believed to have healed a man who had spirit of an unclean devil. Nearby is the Tabgha Church, which was originally called Heptapegon (meaning "seven springs"). This is the site where the miracle of the multiplication of five loaves of bread and two fishes had taken place. It is said that a crowd of 5,000 people, who had assembled here to hear Jesus, were fed due to the multiplication process of the available five loaves of bread and two fishes. Therefore, the Tabgha Church is also referred to as the Church of loaves and fish or the Church of multiplication. Then visited the nearby Church of Beatitudes, meaning ultimate bliss, built by Roman Catholics at the site of delivery of the famed Sermon on the Mount by Jesus. The church is octagonal in shape signifying eight beatitudes which are prudence, fortitude, temperance, justice, humility, faith, hope and charity. These eight beatitudes referred to by Jesus are given in the Gospel of St. Matthews (5: 3-10) as quoted below:

1. Blessed are the poor in spirit,
    for theirs is the kingdom of heaven.

2. Blessed are they who mourn,
   for they shall be comforted.
3. Blessed are the meek,
   for they shall inherit the earth.
4. Blessed are they who hunger and thirst for righteousness,
   for they shall be satisfied.
5. Blessed are the merciful,
   for they shall obtain mercy.
6. Blessed are the poor of heart,
   for they shall see God.
7. Blessed are the peacemakers,
   for they shall be called children of God.
8. Blessed are they who are persecuted for the sake of righteousness,
   for theirs is the kingdom of heaven.

All the eight beatitudes are positive and provide a way of life that promises salvation and provide peace in the midst of trials and tribulations on this earth. Jesus gives message of humility, charity and brotherly love. He teaches transformation of the inner person. He presents beatitudes in positive sense as virtues in life which will ultimately lead to reward. They promise salvation not in this world, but in the next.

In contrast, "The Ten Commandments" by Moses are mostly negative in the sense that these are evils one must avoid in daily life on earth, as most of the Ten

Commandments start with the prefix "Thou shalt not" or "Thou shalt have/do no".

Proceeded to the nearby Church of Primacy of Peter, where Jesus had bestowed Peter with his authority. Also, nearby in the Mensa Christ Church, there is a commemorative table known as "Mensa Christ" wherein "The Last Supper" is believed to have taken place.

Capernaum, Tabgha Church of loaves and fishes, Church of Beatitudes (of Sermon on the Mount), Church of Primacy of Peter and Mensa Christ Church are all close to each other in a vast complex. After visiting all these in the complex, at the adjacent Peter Restaurant, had lunch with a big fried mackerel fish called Peter fish, which was part of the menu.

Day 2: Afternoon

In the afternoon, visited the Wedding Church at Cana on the shore of Sea of Galilee where the first miracle was performed by Jesus. During the wedding feast attended by Mary with Jesus, the wine ran out. On the plea by Mary, Jesus turned the water in a large pot into wine. Near the Wedding Church is the rock on which Jesus was sitting early one morning watching Simon Peter, James and Andrew trying to catch fish. They could not get any fish from the sea during the whole night. Jesus told them to cast the fishing net to the opposite side of the boat. They got a mighty catch of fish. Thereafter, proceeded to Jordan valley of Tiberias and stopped at Yardenit, the site of baptism of Jesus by John, the Baptist.

The actual site of baptism of Jesus by John, the Baptist, was in Qasr al -Yahud which is to the north of Dead Sea and east of Jericho. But after the six-day war of 1967, this site became a frontier area of Israel and Jordan border. Hence in 1981, Israel developed the alternate site at Yardenit, located along the River Jordan at the southern tip of the Sea of Galilee, away from the frontier post. Since then, this baptism site is attracting large number of pilgrim tourists from all over the world. However, in 2011, Israel has reopened the original baptism site of Qasr al -Yahud. But the rush of pilgrims to this original holy site associated with Jesus is not as popular, mainly due to the difficult accessibility of the site on the north of Dead Sea.

Day 3: Forenoon

In the morning, proceeded to Mount Tabor Church of Transfiguration built by Franciscan brothers with three chapels for Moses, Elijah and Jesus. The church is built at the site where Jesus had vision of Moses and Elijah and was transfigured (metamorphized) and Jesus became radiant. The scene was witnessed by Simon Peter, James and John, who heard Jesus being referred to as "He is the chosen one". There is a monastery of the Franciscan brothers nearby. From Mount Tabor an aerial view of Armageddon is possible in the valley below. Armageddon is believed to be the site where the final apocalypse is to take place, as per "Revelations" book of New Testament.

Proceeded on a long drive to Haifa, the largest port city of Israel, near the slopes of Mount Carmel. The

Carmelite monastery of St. Elijah (Stella Maris) is located on these slopes. Their nuns remain in total isolation within the monastery throughout the year and come out of the monastery only once in a year. The famous beautiful Bahai Hanging Gardens in terraced form and the Bahai shrine are also located on these slopes. Had lunch in a restaurant near Bahai shrine.

Day 3: Afternoon

Drove through Jaffa and Tel Aviv, the financial centre of Israel where most of the foreign embassies, missions and consulates are located. The driveway is along the Mediterranean Sea where the hugely popular beaches can be viewed. On the way, stopped at the city of Caesarea ruins and the beach. The city was built by Herod, the Great, who ruled Rome when Jesus was born. The ruins of the aqueduct built for bringing water to the city can be seen. Proceeded further to Ein Kareem, the city of Judah and the birthplace of John, the Baptist, who was son of Elizabeth (cousin of Mary) and Zachariah. The famous Church of Visitation in ruins can be seen here. The church honours the visit of Mary to Elizabeth and Zachariah. By evening/nightfall, reached hotel in Bethlehem in Jerusalem for duration of stay for the remaining part of the tour in Israel.

Day 4: Forenoon

In the morning, proceeded to Kiryat Arba Hebron in Palestine area where tombs of the patriarchs of Jews are located side by side. These tombs are of Abraham, Sarah, Isaac, Jacob, Rebekah and Leah. Nearby, there are parallel tombs side by side of Ibrahim, Hagar, Ishmael etc who are considered to be their patriarchs by Muslims.

Jewish settlements in Palestine are separated from the Arab Muslim neighbourhood. Though the Muslims reside in the neighbourhood, they cannot set up business there and are not permitted to use any vehicle. The atmosphere is always tense in these areas.

Proceeded to the City of David in Bethlehem in Judah province where the Church of Nativity is located near Manager Square. This is the birthplace of Jesus and is the holiest place for Christians. The place receives the largest number of pilgrim visitors every day with crowd control being a nightmare. There are three major churches here which belong to Greek Orthodox, Armenian Orthodox and Roman Catholics (represented by the Franciscan Order). The churches are approached through three gates and for the last 800 years two Muslim families here are vested with the responsibility of safekeeping of the keys which are used to open the three gates. There are three minor churches or chapels as well belonging to Syrian Orthodox, Ethiopian Orthodox and Coptic Church of Egypt. Coptics are Egyptian Christians belonging to Coptic Church which was established in Alexandria, Egypt by St. Mark between 42 and 62 CE. The Star of David in a grotto here signifies the birthplace of Jesus. There is no place for Protestants and Anglicans in Church of Nativity.

Later, visited Shepherds Field near the cloister of grottos of the tombs of St Jerome and Rachel. It is in these fields that David tended his flock of sheep until he was anointed as King of Israel. During the reign of King Herod, the Archangel Gabriel announced the birth of Jesus to the shepherds of the field here.

Day 4: Afternoon

In the afternoon, proceeded to visit the surviving section of the Western Wailing Wall by passing through the Jewish quarter of the old city of Jerusalem. The Wailing Wall is considered to be the holiest and most sacred place for the Jews. Spent some time watching the wall, with many from our group and other pilgrims, going to the wall and praying. Then, through an adjacent barricaded corridor, entered the area where the two mosques are located on the other side of the Western Wailing Wall. Here the mosque of black rock, dome of chain and mosque of golden dome are located, all close to each other in a huge compound complex. Other than Muslims, none is allowed to enter the mosques. When Jews move around in the compound, many Muslims could be seen shouting, to express their anger against the Jews.

Beyond the golden domed mosque, there is an open area below which can be seen a closed gate through which Jesus had entered the temple area. Three pools called the North pool, the South pool and the Israeli pool can be seen below from this open area. It is said that at the North pool a crippled man had sat for 38 years and Jesus had sprinkled the holy water from the pool on him and he was cured. The Israeli pool is used for sacrifice of goats.

Day 5: Forenoon

In the morning, proceeded to the Mount of Olives which offers a panoramic view of Jerusalem. Mount of Olives and Mount Zion are opposite to each other with a valley in between. On Mount Zion at the Temple Mount, Solomon had built the first temple, over which today stands the mosque of black rock. Next to it is the mosque of Al Aqsa with the golden dome. At Mount of Olives is the Church of Ascension where there is a footprint of Jesus. It is believed that after resurrection, Jesus appeared at least on 10 different occasions at various places. He appeared to Mary Magdalene in Jerusalem with a spade in his hands, initially making her believe he was a gardener. He appeared to the pilgrims from various countries, who had assembled in Mount Zion on the occasion of Pentecost. The pilgrims felt that the spirit of Jesus had enveloped them and they started talking in their various languages. They were then addressed by St. Peter. Jesus also appeared to his disciples at Galilee and the mountain. It is believed that after 40 days from the day of resurrection, he finally ascended to heaven from the site of the Church of Ascension at Mount of Olives, the footprint here signifying the event.

There is a steep descent from Mount of Olives known as Palm Sunday road leading to the Garden of Gethsemane. Palm Sunday is the Sunday before the Friday crucifixion of Jesus when he had walked down this road. Palm Sunday road was so named as palm branches were strewn in front of Jesus by his followers on his walk down the descent for his entry into Jerusalem. On this descent along the slope, stopped at the sanctuary/church of Pater Noster Ascension and the chapel of Dominus Flavit. The chapel of Dominus Flavit has been built in the shape of a tear drop as a poignant reminder to the fact that Jesus had shed tears here over the imminent destruction of Jerusalem and the temple. On the side of Palm Sunday road there are tombs of ancient Jews. The tombs are over ground with a stone slab cover over them so that on the Day of Judgement to be held in the valley with the resurrection of Jesus, yet to come, the buried Jews may go to heaven.

At the end of Palm Sunday road there is Garden of Gethsemane where the Church of Gethsemane is located. This church is also known as the Church of Agony since it is believed that "The Last Supper" which Jesus had with his 12 disciples had taken place at this site. The church has stands with black images depicting "The Last Supper" of Jesus with his 12 disciples. The church is also often referred to as the Church of all nations (18 nations in all). It is so called as it was built with the contribution of the poor Roman Catholics of 18 nations, with no contribution forthcoming from any of the rich Christian nations.

Following the last supper, Jesus was walking in the garden of olives which is just outside the church. During this walk, he was suddenly arrested by the soldiers of King Herod and taken away. The garden has an olive tree which is reputed to be 2,200 years old. The garden also has many olive trees which are hundreds of years old.

At the bottom of the slope of Palm Sunday road there is a church called Church of Mary Magdalene which can be reached by descending 45 steps. The tomb of Mary Magdalene is empty signifying her journey or assumption to heaven. Near the church, stands the Milk Grotto where Mother Mary is feeding baby Jesus. The grotto walls are coloured milky white.

Day 5: Afternoon

In the afternoon, proceeded to Dead Sea, known as Megilot Dead Sea, through a mountainous road which has steep gradients and many tunnels on the way. The Dead Sea is the lowest point on earth at 400 m (1,312 ft) below sea level. Sea of Galilee itself is 209 m (686 ft) below sea level. On the northwest bank of Dead Sea are located the Qumran (Comaron) caves. In 1946/47, from one of these caves, some Bedouin shepherds discovered the first Dead Sea scrolls written on dried goatskin. The site of these caves was turned into an archaeological site from where the archaeologists discovered more of the scrolls as the search continued till 1956. These scrolls gave valuable historical information on the Jews written by the ancient writers. Translations of these are available now in many languages of the world.

The Dead Sea is very rich in minerals such as potash, salt, potassium, magnesium etc which have given rise to many industries manufacturing cosmetic products. Most of these products are beneficial to people with skin diseases.

There is a popular beach called Kaliah beach where many pilgrim visitors can be seen floating on the salty buoyant water of Dead Sea. Due to the buoyant property of the salty water one cannot drown here. Many of them can be seen rubbing the soil from the shallow sea bed on their skin due to its healing property.

Day 6: Forenoon

In the morning, proceeded to Garden Tom which is considered by the Protestants and the Anglicans to be the true place of crucifixion, burial and resurrection of Jesus. The Skull Rock can be viewed on one side of the garden. There is a cellar in the garden which is claimed to be the burial chamber of Jesus. The Protestants and Anglicans believe that Jesus had journeyed to heaven and therefore the tomb is empty. At the chamber it is inscribed – "He is not there, for he is risen". However, this theory or contention is disputed and disbelieved by most people as the evidence of Jesus having been buried at the Church of the Holy Sepulchre in Jerusalem is too very overwhelming.

Proceeded to the old city of Jerusalem at Mount Zion to "Via Dolorosa" (meaning "Way of Grief"), which is traditionally accepted as the last route trodden by Jesus while being taken to the Cross of Golgotha (in Aramaic) or "The Skull" or Calvary in English, where the crucifixion took place. Starting from Pontius Pilate's Judgement Hall to the

Chapel of Flagellation (where the Roman soldiers scourged Jesus and placed a crown of thorns on his head), to the arch constructed by Emperor Hadrian, to the Convent of the Sisters of Zion (below which are the Lithotrities where Jesus was publicly tried and the Roman soldiers mocked him), to the 14 stations on the route to the Cross are called the Way of Grief. The last five stations are inside the Church of the Holy Sepulchre with its two silver domes and "The Tomb", believed to be part of the stone slab that covered the tomb of Jesus. The Church of the Holy Sepulchre, also called the Church of Resurrection, was constructed in 325-326 CE by Emperor Constantine, the Great, along with his mother Helena (after they both embraced Christianity in 313 CE). The church was constructed over a temple built by the Roman Emperor Hadrian in 2nd century CE over the purported cave tomb where Jesus was buried. The Church of the Holy Sepulchre is considered to be the holiest place in Christendom, located in the Christian Quarter of the old city of Jerusalem in Temple Mount, only a little distance away from the mosque of golden dome of Al Aqsa.

Visited the nearby Dormition Abbey which is under the management of Benedictines of Rome. Dormition stands for the passing away of Mary from earthly life to heaven, which according to Roman Catholic Church is called Assumption. An annual feast is held on 15th August to commemorate this. In the "Upper Room" of Dormition Abbey is the tomb of King David covered with a blue cloth with many images in Hebrew and a violin. However, there are many who are sceptical about the remains of David being within this tomb as it is believed that all the Israeli kings were buried in tunnel tombs in the City of David, south of the old city of Jerusalem. It is believed that both David and Solomon were buried in these tunnel tombs which were damaged at a later period due to quarrying.

Proceeded further for a visit to the Church of St. Peter of Gallicantu, which symbolizes Peter's denial of Jesus, as was prophesied by Jesus himself during "The Last Supper". The next visit was to the house of the high priest Caiaphas, where Jesus was imprisoned in a dungeon on Thursday, the night before crucifixion. Caiaphas was the infamous high priest who was the leader of conspiracy to crucify Jesus.

Day 6: Afternoon

In the afternoon visited the Mount of Precipice, also known as the Mount of Precipitation/Mount of the Lord/Mount Kedurmin. It is located just outside Nazareth. It is believed to be the site of "Rejection of Jesus", when the people of Nazareth refused to accept Jesus as a Messiah and tried to push him off down the mountain. But Jesus just passed through the midst of the crowd and went away.

Proceeded to Jericho in the old city of Jerusalem. Carbon tests have confirmed Jericho to be 12,000 years old, thus making it the oldest living city in the world. Jericho is the place where Jesus stopped on his way to Jerusalem on the eve of Passover and cured a blind man during his stay at the house of Zachaeus. . At Jericho there is a cable car station. A 1,300 m long cable car service takes one to the limestone mountain northwest of Jericho called Quarantal, where the Orthodox Church has established a monastery. The cable car ride is an optional one on payment. The limestone mountain is part of Mountain of Temptation located in Judaeau desert. The Mount of Temptation is so named as Jesus had spent 40 days there in prayer and penance before his crucifixion and the devil had unsuccessfully tempted him during this period. Near the cable station at Jericho, there is a supermarket. In the compound of the supermarket, there is a spring which continues to flow. It is called Elijah's spring. It is believed that when Elijah was moving in the desert, he became quite thirsty and he struck on the slope of earth here. A fresh water spring sprouted from the spot whose perennial flow of fresh drinking water is continuing even today. Many beautiful peacocks and peahens can be seen strutting around nearby.

Next was a visit to the tomb of Lazarus located at Bethany in Jerusalem. Lazarus was an ardent devotee of Jesus. On the death of Lazarus, his two sisters Mary and Martha, sent word across to Jesus to visit them. Upon arrival of Jesus, the two sisters earnestly pleaded with him to revive their brother who was dead for a few days. Jesus called Lazarus to wake up and he revived. The site of the tomb of Lazarus was occupied by Al-Uzair mosque since 16th century under Ottoman rule. In the 1950's, a Roman Catholic Church of the Franciscan Order and in the 1960's, a Greek Orthodox Church have been built nearby. The site is thus sacred to both Christians and Muslims alike.

Day 7 0.

In the morning, left Jerusalem towards Dead Sea. From Dead Sea, travelled from north to south by highway that runs parallel to the shore which lies on east side. The west side of the highway is mountainous with numerous caves and canyons. With frequent rains, mudslides from the canyons are quite common on the highway, making it slippery and dangerous, at times even blocking the highway. In this desert area of Negev, there are many nature parks on the east between Dead Sea and the highway with deer, ostrich etc. Also, on the east, there are many factories processing the minerals from the Dead Sea for commercial production. Many pipelines also can be seen running parallel to the highway conveying oil from Eilat port to Tel Aviv. Many cars from Japan and South Korea and many goods, all imported at Eilat port, can be seen being transported by huge trucks by this highway to Israel and through Israel to European countries. This highway is a lifeline of Israel and remains quite busy all the time.

Statue of Lot's wife

Sodom and Gomorrah were cities near Dead Sea which were destroyed by fire and brimstone during the biblical times due to God's wrath on the sinners there. Lot who lived here was a pure and God-fearing person. During the destruction of the two sin-cities, two angels took Lot, his wife and their daughters out of the city and fled to the hills. The angels told them not to look back while fleeing. Despite this warning, Lot's wife looked back and instantly turned into a salt statue/pillar. On the hillside on the west (right side of the highway) on Mount Sodom, the white salt statue is clearly visible from a distance when the visibility is good.

Reached Eilat port area which is on the mouth of Gulf of Aqaba. There is an airport also at Eilat. Eilat is a very important city of Israel through which most of the imported goods are received from the Asian countries on the east. Eilat has been developed as a popular seaside resort with many premier hotels, malls and shopping centres. Immediately after Eilat is the Menachem Begin land border check post between Israel and Egypt at Taba. Taba is at the north-eastern tip of Sinai Peninsula of Egypt. From Taba onward the road runs parallel to the Gulf of Aqaba all the way down to the southernmost tip of the gulf at Sharm el Sheikh. Midway on this road, there is a road which goes into Sinai Peninsula to a city called St. Catherine where one halts for the night stay in a hotel.

Day 8

In the morning, proceeded to St. Catherine Monastery located on Mount Sinai, also called Mount of Moses. Leading his followers from Egypt and crossing the Red Sea, Moses entered Sinai and proceeded ahead. He is believed to have left his followers at a place. He instructed them to wait for him there and went up Mount Sinai to seek guidance from God. As the followers had to wait for many days, they lost their patience and faith in Moses and God. At the place where they halted, there was a cave mould, into which molten gold was poured by the followers of

Moses to make a golden bull calf with a head and legs. Then, they started worshipping this golden bull calf. This cave is visible at the foot of Mount Sinai, where we halted. After 40 days of praying to God on Mount Sinai, Moses received the tablets of "The Ten Commandments" from God and returned to his followers. Some distance ahead is the St. Catherine Monastery. As the last stretch to the monastery is not navigable to buses, the pilgrims have to cover the distance either by taxis or by foot. The monastery is located in a cave, outside which is the chapel of "Burning Bush", through which God is believed to have communicated to Moses while giving him the tablets of the ten commandments. The monastery is run by nuns of St. Catherine. In the 4th century CE, Catherine lived in Alexandria in Egypt and was put to death for her preaching of Christianity, thus becoming a martyr. Angels are believed to have carried her remains to Mount Sinai. Some monks from Sinai monastery found these remains and a monastery for nuns was built at this place in the 6th century CE by Emperor Justinian with a chapel of the "Burning Bush". St. Catherine has a small airfield where pilgrims and tourists can land directly, avoiding the circuitous and hazardous long land route.

From St. Catherine, taking the road back to the coastal road along the shores of Gulf of Aqaba, the pilgrims proceed down to Sharm el Sheikh at the tip of the peninsula. This part of the road passes through wild and barren mountainous terrain, sparsely populated by Arab Bedouins. These Bedouins with their camels often attack the buses with pilgrims and tourists and the trucks carrying goods. They loot the goods and often take the bus passengers as hostages demanding ransom. In February, 2014, the Bedouins blasted a pilgrim tourist bus near the border check post of Taba, killing some South Korean pilgrims and injuring many passengers. Since then the Egyptian government has introduced the combo convoy system for movement of vehicles for the safety and security of pilgrims, tourists and vehicles on this route. In this procedure, the movement of vehicles is controlled by allowing a convoy of buses, cars and trucks accompanied by armed police/military vehicles escorting them. The convoys leave every four hours or so. Due to the many check posts on the way and the requirement of obtaining road clearances, the journey takes long hours causing delays, particularly if a tourist bus misses the combo convoy.

The Sinai Peninsula is a sparsely inhabited terrain in Negev desert with very poor road communication and infrastructure facilities. But it is very rich in minerals which are yet to be surveyed, assessed and explored. That is why Israel was keen to retain Sinai Peninsula after it had annexed it during the six-day war in 1967. However, Israel had to return Sinai to Egypt as per the Camp David Accord.

The lunch halt was at Sharm el Sheikh, which is considered to be the Paris of Egypt with many luxury hotels, restaurants, casinos, nightclubs, beautiful beaches dotted with palm trees with scuba diving, snorkeling and other facilities, attracting plenty of holiday makers and international tourists. There are many military training establishments at Sharm el Sheikh. The road from here turns northwards along the coast of Red Sea and is well maintained. It proceeds smoothly through a township of Dahab on the way and near Suez port enters a tunnel to cross Red Sea to enter the periphery of Cairo. Through the chaotic traffic of vehicles, the bus reaches a hotel in Giza plateau on the west bank of River Nile for the night halt.

Day 9

In the morning, proceeded to the top of Giza plateau to visit the Three Great Pyramids. The first item in the itinerary list of any tourist visiting Cairo, is the Great Pyramids of Giza, known as the Giza Necropolis. The three pyramids are of the Pharaohs, Cheops, Chepren and Mycerinus. The pyramids are guarded by the mysterious Sphinx, a mythical statue with the body of a lion and the head of a human. These three pyramids facing the ancient city of Cairo are the only surviving ones of the original seven wonders of the ancient world.

After the pyramids, visited the nearby scent factory, papyrus show room and Egyptian cotton clothes store.

The second item in the itinerary of the tourist visitor is the famous archaeological museum of Egypt containing the great treasures of the buried Pharaohs of Egypt. But the site of the museum was at the opposite end of the Giza plateau. To reach the museum from Giza, the tourist had to go right across the city of Cairo, negotiating through the incredibly chaotic and heavy traffic of Cairo roads. The old museum site was near the famous Tahrir square which was the scene of massive protest demonstrations, called the Arab Spring in 2012. The protests were against the dictator Hosni Mubarak who had been ruling Egypt for many decades with an iron fist. The open large square can accommodate many thousands of people who had converged there and stayed put for days. The square later on was heavily guarded by military personnel with tanks to ward off any further public flare up.

For the last many years, the process of shifting of the exhibit treasures of the museum from Tahrir site to Giza site near the Great Pyramids, has been going on. The new site is about 2 kms from the Great Pyramids, so that a visitor can conveniently cover both without much of inconvenience. With an ultra-modern grand building, the new museum is getting readied for inauguration during end of 2022. The Grand Egyptian Museum (GEM) will be the largest archaeological museum in the world

End of Pilgrimage. In Jerusalem, King Herod was informed by his oracle that his enemy was already born. Hearing this prediction, the angry, ruthless king decreed that all infants in his kingdom be killed. Archangel Gabriel gave instructions to Joseph to flee from Israel. Accordingly, Joseph and Mary with baby Jesus, fled from Bethlehem to Egypt and lived in Egypt in many places for three years and then returned to Nazareth.

In old Cairo, visited the Abu Serga Coptic Church, also called Saints Sergius and Bacchus Church, in the cave. This was the site where the holy family lived for some period after they fled from Israel. Visited nearby St. George Cathedral and monastery which were built to commemorate this event. Also, visited a cavern church nearby which has a well, used by Mother Mary to draw water.

The evening was spent on a pleasant leisurely cruise on River Nile with dinner, accompanied by an entertainment programme consisting of the famous Arabian belly dancers, whirling dervish dancers, puppet shows and magic tricks.

Proceeded to Cairo airport to catch a flight to homeland.

Conclusion

The Middle East/West Asia region has been historically experiencing conflicts, skirmishes, flare ups and wanton killings of innocent inhabitants. In the recent past, indoctrination by fundamentalists and recruitment to terrorist organizations have been on the increase. In this cruel process, fleeing of persecuted people to other countries and many of them succumbing to death and injuries have been widely reported. It is a human tragedy of Herculean proportions. The various agencies of United Nations and the Western nations have not been successful in negotiating any lasting solution for establishing peace in the region.

A study of the basic teachings of scriptures of any religion will convince anyone that no faith or religion preaches hatred or persecution of other believers. To live peacefully, harmoniously and compassionately, helping the less fortunate in their miseries and times of need, is what any religion professes. However, there are many in any religion or society, who have their own selfish agenda in creating misinterpretation of religious texts, misinforming and misguiding the gullible lay public to create misunderstanding against others. The sane elements present in every religion or society have a duty to come forward, expose these mischief makers, isolate them and show the right path to the lay public.

Hoping that this book may create an awareness to such personnel to give proper guidance to the gullible lay people, with the proliferation of online platforms, which are accessible to anyone interested.

Bibliography

1. ARMSTRONG, KAREN.: A History of God: The 4,000 Year Quest of Judaism, Christianity and Islam, New York, Ballantine Books, Published by The Random House Publishing Group, 1991

2. GUNTER, STEMBERGER.; Jews and Christians in the Holy Land: Palestine in the Fourth Century, Bloomsbury Publishing, 1999

3. PROTHERO, STEPHEN.: God is not One: The Eight Rival Religions That Run the World, 2010

4. HOPFE, LEWIS M.; WOODWARD, MARK R.: Religions of the World, Arizona State University, 1976

5. ROBINSON, THOMAS A.; RODRIGUES, HILLARY P.: World Religions: A Guide to the Essentials, Baker Academic, 2006

6. PARTRIDGE, CHRISTOPHER.: Introduction to World religions, 2005

7. FEATURED RELIGIONS AND BELIEFS: bbc.co.uk/religions, 2014

8. THE HISTORY OF ISRAELITES – FROM THE BIBLE UNTIL TODAY; www.considerthegospel.org

9. HISTORY OF ISRAEL AND THE JEWS – FROM ABRAHAM TO MODERN DAY; www.en.shalomfromg – d.net/jewish history/bible-to-today

10. ANTI-SEMITISM: HISTORY, FACTS AND EXAMPLES – BRITANNICA; WWW.britannica.com

11. NAZI ANTI-SEMITISM AND THE HOLOCAUST – ENCYCLOPEDIA BRITANNICA; www.britannica.com

12. WHAT IS THE DIFFERENCE BETWEEN ANTI-SEMITISM AND ANTI-ZIONISM; www.bbc.com

13. ANTI-ZIONISM-WIKIPEDIA; www.en.wikipedia.org

Glossary

Abel – Son of Adam and Eve

Abu Serga Church – Coptic Church in Egypt commemorating the site where the holy family of Mary, Joseph and baby Jesus lived after fleeing Israel

Al Aqsa – Literally "The farthest", referring to Jerusalem, it is the mosque with golden dome built at Temple Mount

Al-Masjid an-Nabawi – Mosque at Medina where Prophet Muhammad was buried

Aphrodite – Greek goddess of love and beauty

Apollo- Greek god of arts, music, youth and beauty

Apostle – Primary disciple of Jesus

Aramaic – Ancestral language to Hebrew and Arabic

Archangel Gabriel – Guardian angel of Israel, who appears in the Hebrew Bible, New Testament and the Quran (called Jibril)

Armageddon – Site in the valley near Mount Tabor where the final apocalypse is to take place

Ashkenazim – Mixture of Hebrew and German

Ashur – Patron god of Assyrians

Athena – Greek goddess of wisdom, handicraft and warfare

Ayyub dynasty – Formed by descendants of Muhammad in 750 CE after overthrowing the Umayyad dynasty

Bakrid – Festival signifying sacrifice of goat in place of Ishmael by Ibrahim at Temple Mount

Bethany – Location of tomb of Lazarus, an ardent devotee of Jesus

Bethlehem – Place in City of David where Jesus was born

Blue Mosque – Magnificent mosque built by Sultan Ahmed near Hagia Sophia in Istanbul

Byzantium – Emperor Constantine built his imperial residence at Byzantium and renamed it as Constantinople (present-day Istanbul)

Cain – Son of Adam and Eve

Calvary (in English) – Also called "Skull" (in English), it is the place of crucifixion of Jesus

Candelabra – Same as Menorah

Capernaum – Located north of Sea of Galilee, it was the centre of public ministry by Jesus

Catacombs – Underground tunnels in Rome where early Christians lived due to fear of persecution

Church of Agony – Located at Garden of Gethsemane where "The Last Supper" was held

Church of Ascension – Located at Mount of Olives from where Jesus ascended to heaven

Church of Assumption – Located at Dormition Abbey from where Mary ascended to heaven

Church of Beatitude – Site of delivery of address "Sermon on the Mount" by Jesus

Church of Holy Sepulchre – Church built at the site of cave tomb of Jesus at Temple Mount

Church of Mary Magdalene – Church at the end of the slope of Palm Sunday with the empty tomb of Mary Magdalene, signifying her ascent to heaven

Church of Nativity – Located at Bethlehem where Jesus was born and is considered to be the holiest place of Christendom

Church of Primacy of Peter – Site where Jesus bestowed his authority on Peter

Church of St. Peter of Gallicantu – Signifies Peter's denial of Jesus

Church of Visitation – Built in memory of visit by Mary to Elizabeth and Zachariah, parents of John, The Baptist

Cross of Golgotha (in Aramaic) – Place of crucifixion of Jesus

Crusades – Series of holy wars that took place between 1095 and 1230 with Christians fighting battles with Islamic rulers for control of Jerusalem

David – Second king of Israel, composed 150 psalms

Dead Sea – Lowest point on earth at 400 m below sea level, rich in minerals

Gentile – Non-Jewish, non-Christian laymen

Goliath – Giant of Israel, who was killed by David

Gospel – Messenger of God

Hadith – Teachings and normative examples of Muhammad during his lifetime

Hagar/Agar – Egyptian maid of Sarah and became second wife of Abraham

Hagia Sophia – Magnificent church with massive dome built by Emperor Justinian in Istanbul

Haram al Sharif – Literally meaning "Noble sanctuary", it is the mosque with dome of black rock built at Temple Mount

Helios – Greek sun god

Herod, the Great – Vassal ruler under Roman Empire who captured Jerusalem in 38 BCE and enlarged the temple at the Mount

Isaac – Son of Abraham

Ishmael – Son of Abraham

Isra & Miraj – Two parts of a night journey purported to have undertaken by Prophet Muhammad in 621, signifying a physical and spiritual journey to Jerusalem

Jacob – Son of Isaac, who took the name of Israel

Jesus Christ – Christians consider Jesus as their messiah and follow his teachings

John, the Baptist – Ascetic of Judaean desert who baptised Jesus

Joseph – Youngest son of Jacob, rescued and brought up by an Egyptian

Juda/Judah (In Latin and Greek) – Also Juea/Judaea/Judaeau (in Hebrew), Southern kingdom of Israel, whose capital was Jerusalem

Juno – Roman mother goddess, wife of sky god Jupiter

Jupiter – Patron sky god of ancient Romans

Kibbutz – Community living centre of Israel

Kiryat Arba Hebron – Place of tombs of Patriarchs of Abrahamic religions

Madaba – 3500 year- old city of mosaics in Amman, Jordan

Magen David – Meaning "Shield of David" and popularly called Star of David, it is the symbol of Israel

Maimonides – 13 Articles of Faith written by Malmonides, famous Jewish philosopher/scholar

Mamluks – Muslims who controlled Jerusalem from 1291 to 1511

Mardak – Patron god of Babylonians

Mary Magdalene – A close follower of Jesus and was witness to his crucifixion and was the first one to see him after resurrection

Masjid al Haram – Grand mosque in Mecca where Hajj is performed

Menorah – Also called candelabra, it is a six-branched candle tree lamp stand used for worship in ancient times by Jews

Mensa Church – Site where "The Last Supper" is believed to have been held

Milk Grotto – Mother Mary feeding baby Jesus in grotto with walls coloured milky white, near Church of Mary Magdalene

Minerva – Roman goddess of wisdom, intelligence and handicraft

Mount Carmel – Site of Monastery of St. Elijah (Stella Mary) and Hanging Gardens and Shrine of Bahai'

Mount Nebo – Mount in Jordan where Moses was given the vision of "Promised land" of Israel by God

Mount of Precipice/Precipitation – Located at Nazareth where "Rejection of Jesus" by people took place

Mount of Temptation – Located near Jericho where Jesus spent 40 days in prayer and penance and devil unsuccessfully tried to tempt him

Mount Tabor – Site of Church where "Transfiguration of Jesus" took place as witnessed by his disciples

Mustafa Kemal Ataturk – Turkey Army officer and revolutionary, who modernised Turkey into a secular democratic state in 1924

Naamah – Egyptian queen wife of Solomon

Nazareth – Boyhood town of Jesus in Jerusalem

Nehemiah – Completed second temple at Jerusalem

Noah's Ark – Ark built by pious, old Noah on God's order, for rescuing mankind, animals and birds from the great deluge in ancient period

Osiris – Egyptian god of underworld

Palm Sunday – Steep descent from Mount of Olives to Garden of Gethsemane, trodden by Jesus on the Sunday before his crucifixion on Friday

Pentateuch – Also called Torah, Original 5 books of Judaism authored by Moses

Qasr al -Yahud – Traditionally believed to be the baptismal site, located north of Dead Sea and east of Jericho, where Jesus was baptised by John, the Baptist

Queen Sheba – Queen of neighbouring country of Israel, known for her striking beauty

Qumran – Also called "Comaron", these are caves near Dead Sea where the scrolls were discovered in 1946/47

Ra – Patron sun god of ancient Egyptians

Ramses – Prince son of Pharaoh, builder of Egyptian pyramid

Roma – Roman goddess who personifies Roman state and city

Samaria – Capital of Northern kingdom of Israel

Sarah – Wife of Abraham

Saul – First king of Israel

Sea of Galilee – Sea separating Israel from Jordan

Semitic – Relating or denoting to the peoples who speak languages of Hebrew, Aramaic, Phoenician etc

Sephardim – Mixture of Hebrew and Spanish

Shepherds Field – Fields where David tended his flock of sheep before he was anointed King of Israel

Solomon – Son and successor king to David, known for his wisdom

Star of David – Symbol of Israel

Sura – Chapter of Quran

Tabgha Church – Church on shore of Sea of Galilee where miracle of multiplication of 5 loaves and 2 fish took place

Talmud – Literally "Learning", Jewish scripture consisthng of Mishnah and Gemara

Tanakh – Hebrew Bible

Torah – Also called Pentateuch, Original 5 books of Judaism authored by Moses

Venus – Roman goddess of love

Via Dolorosa – Meaning "Way of grief", it is traditionally accepted as the last route trodden by Jesus before crucifixion

Wailing Wall – Wall at Temple Mount, most sacred place for Jews, where they wail on the destruction of the Temple

Waqf Board – Legal institution of charitable trust

Wedding Church – At Cana on shore of Sea of Galilee where miracle of turning of water into wine was performed by Jesus during a wedding

Yardenit – Alternate baptismal site developed by modern Israel, located along River Jordan, at the southern tip of Sea of Galilee, for commemorating baptism of Jesus by John, the Baptist

Yom Kippur – Day of atonement for fasting and praying by Jews

Zerubbabel – Completed second temple at Jerusalem

Zeus – Greek god of sun and thunder

Zionism – Pursuit of an independent Israeli state

Index

A

Abel, 21, 47, 113, 123

Abu Serga Church, 113, 123

Al Aqsa, 40-41, 81, 94, 98, 113, 123

Al-Masjid an-Nabawi, 113, 123

Aphrodite, 19, 113, 123

Apollo, 19, 113, 123

Apostle, 30, 59, 113, 123

Aramaic, 34, 53, 56, 97, 113, 115, 120, 123

Archangel Gabriel, 28, 87, 93, 106, 113, 123

Armageddon, 90, 113, 123

Ashkenazim, 57, 114, 123

Ashur, 19, 114, 123

Athena, 19, 114, 123

Ayyub dynasty, 114, 123

B

Bakrid, 22, 49, 114, 123

Bethany, 100, 114, 123

Bethlehem, 28-29, 91-92, 106, 114-115, 123

Blue Mosque, 43, 114, 123

Byzantium, 33, 114, 123

C

Cain, 21, 47, 114, 123

Calvary, 97, 114, 123

Candelabra, 72-73, 114, 118, 123

Capernaum, 87, 89, 114, 123

Catacombs, 33, 114, 123

Church of Agony, 95, 115, 123

Church of Ascension, 31, 94, 115, 123